Year 2/Primary 3

Including
Lower-achievers
in the
Maths
Lesson

Maureen Nixon
Sue Atkinson

HOPSCOTCH
EDUCATIONAL PUBLISHING

Contents

Published by
Hopscotch Educational Publishing Ltd,
29 Waterloo Place,
Leamington Spa CV32 5LA
Tel: 01926 744227

© 2001 Hopscotch Educational Publishing

Written by Maureen Nixon and Sue Atkinson
Series design by Blade Communications
Illustrated by Bernard Connors
Printed by Clintplan, Southam

ISBN 1-902239-56-3

Maureen Nixon and Sue Atkinson hereby assert their moral right to be identified as the authors of this work in accordance with the Copyright, Designs and Patents Act, 1988.

The authors would like to thank the many teachers and children from the following schools who trialled these activities:

Upton House School, Windsor, Berkshire

Benyon Primary School, South Ockendon, Essex

St. Joseph's RC Primary School, Stanford le Hope, Essex

West Thurrock Primary School, Thurrock, Essex

Christ Church C of E Primary School, South Croydon

Haymerle Special School, London

Bishop Perrin School, Richmond

Sheen Mount Primary School, Richmond

Summerbee Junior School, Bournemouth, Dorset

St Ives First School, St Ives, Ringwood, Hampshire

Mudeford Junior School, Christchurch, Dorset

Linwood School (Special), Bournemouth, Dorset

In the section on Inclusion, The National Curriculum states that schools have a responsibility to provide a broad and balanced curriculum for all pupils. It sets out three principles that are essential to developing a more inclusive curriculum:

A: Setting suitable learning challenges

B: Responding to pupils' diverse learning needs

C: Overcoming potential barriers to learning and assessment...

Including Lower-achievers in the Maths Lesson is a series of books that gives support for including in the daily maths lesson those children in the class who, for whatever reason, are struggling and therefore often failing.

The books can be used alongside the ***Developing Numeracy Skills*** books also published by Hopscotch Educational Publishing Ltd. You will find a cross-reference to these books on the chart on page 5.

CHAPTER CONTENT

The overall learning objectives

Each chapter has overall learning objectives that are based on the key objectives in the *National Numeracy Strategy Framework for Teaching.*

The grid on page 5 shows where these key objectives are covered within the chapters in this book. The lessons in this Year 2/P3 book are based on the Number Key Objectives for Years 1–4 (P2–5) to be found in the *Framework for Teaching.*

The assessment focus

Each chapter is divided into 'sessions' – a set of activities that might last for one or more days. The assessment focus for each session is based on the key objectives and broken down into competencies that the children are expected to achieve within those key objectives.

An individual assessment chart can be found on pages 127 and 128.

With the whole class

This section includes activities that are suitable for everyone in the class but they focus on the work for the lower-achievers that follows. Therefore they use easy numbers so that the lower-achievers can cope

with the maths concept being taught.

You can repeat the whole-class starter(s) over several days or choose another starter that focuses on a similar learning objective.

Some suggested vocabulary is given, but you should teach with your *National Numeracy Strategy Mathematical Vocabulary* to hand.

With the lower-achievers

These are activities that follow on from the whole-class starter and you can use them:

● in the middle of the lesson for children who are under-achieving

● during the next week or two to consolidate the concepts

● when you come back to that topic next term.

Within this section is a selection of activities, some to be done with adult guidance and some which can be done by selected children independently.

With adult support

Many of the activities require equipment. We use equipment so that we are developing the children's mental images and things such as number lines, 100 squares and cubes are absolutely crucial. Many of the activities are games as these can motivate and keep the children involved. You will need to train your children to play games if they are not used to them.

Once taught, some of these activities can be teacher-independent. Often there are examples of questions and other things to say to the children so that their vocabulary is extended.

In addition to the adult support during the activities, try to plan for times when an adult can give a few minutes 'catch up' time to a group of children at odd moments during the day, for example five minutes at the end of assembly or at the start or end of the day. (If possible, take children from more than one class for 'catch up' times to make the best use of the time of an adult helper.)

Teacher-independent activities

These activities are suitable for lower-achievers to do on their own, depending how well they work independently. Again, many of them will require the use of maths equipment.

Plenary session

In this section a few questions are included to help lower-achievers reflect on their work, and sometimes there is an additional activity. Many of the whole-class starters can also be used as activities here.

Keep plenary sessions varied and interesting. They are times to sort out misconceptions, and times to generalise about what has been done. They are not just 'show and tell' times!

The photocopiable resource sheets

Some of the activities suggested in the teachers' notes require the use of resource sheets. A minimum of words is used on these, so helpers will need to have instructions on what to ask the children to do on them. Many of the sheets are blanks, requiring the teacher or adult to write in tasks at a suitable level of ability.

On the more complex sheets for younger children there is a space at the bottom that contains notes for the adult. Sometimes this space is blank. This has been done deliberately as the teacher or adult may wish to add a few notes for another adult to use with a specific child or group. Likewise the sheets may be sent home to the parents/carers and this space can be used for instructions to them.

Some of the artwork on the resource sheets is on the same theme as the *Developing Numeracy Skills* books. However, some of it is more varied to provide interest for the children. We have also provided 'clip art' sheets at the end of the resource sheet section, so that you can cut and stick pictures onto the children's sheets in order to change the appearance of the sheets when you want to use them more than once. This gives the sheets new life and gives the children plenty of practice to consolidate.

A general point about using the sheets with lower-achievers

Although the resource sheets provided in this book can be used several times, remember that it isn't recording maths that is important; it is whether the child can understand the concept. So use the sheets only when they are needed, such as for a teacher-independent activity or for assessment.

Spinners

Some of the games in the book need a spinner that works by trapping a paper-clip in the middle of the spinner then flicking the paper-clip round with a finger. Spinners are quieter than dice and give more choice.

Number lines

Have a large wall number line and 100 square up in each class. Remember that 100 squares are suitable for looking at patterns, such as for 10's, but are not ideal to do calculations on because children tend to get lost as they move from the end of one line to the start of the next. Number lines are much easier to use for calculations.

And finally, remember

We want children to feel positive and to feel that they are achieving well in maths. Working endlessly on activity sheets can be boring, and could even make a child feel they are failing. Use games where possible to reinforce concepts and skills. Be generous with praise.

This grid is made up of the key objectives for Reception/P1, Year 1/P2 and Year 2/P3 plus other crucial learning. It shows the chapter/s where these objectives are covered in this book. The grid also shows where the same area of learning can be found in the *Developing Numeracy Skills* series.

KEY OBJECTIVES	CHAPTERS	DNS – BOOK/CHAPTER
Say and use the number names in order counting forward and back to 20, and count 10/20 objects	1	Year 2 – Chapters 1 and 2
Read and write whole numbers in figures and words to 10/20/100	1, 2	Year 2 – Chapters 1 and 2
Count on and back in 1's and 10's to and from zero (then 5's)	1, 2, 3, 4, 6	Year 2 – Chapters 1 and 3
Describe and extend number sequences including recognising odd and even numbers and multiples of 2, 5 and 10	1, 4, 6	Year 2 – Chapters 1 and 3
Say a number that is 1 or 10 more or less	1, 2	Year 2 – Chapter 2
Use the language of comparing and ordering numbers	2	Year 2 – Chapters 1 and 2
Understand addition and subtraction as counting on and counting back on a number line and use the related vocabulary	3, 4, 5, 6	Year 2 – Chapters 1 and 4
Know by heart all pairs of numbers with a total of 10 (later 20)	3, 4, 5	
Use a range of strategies for addition and subtraction	3, 4, 5	Year 2 – Chapters 4, 5 and 6
Understand the operations of addition and subtraction, using the +, – and = signs	3, 4	Year 2 – Chapters 4 and 5
Put the larger number first when adding	3	Year 2 – Chapter 4
Know all doubles to 5 and recognise near doubles	3, 5, 6	
Use a number line to add 10 and then add 9	3, 5	Year 2 – Chapter 6
Use patterns of similar calculations	3, 4, 5	Year 2 – Chapter 7
Find a total when one group of objects is hidden and use symbols to stand for an unknown number	5	Year 2 – Chapter 4
Understand multiplication as repeated addition or as describing an array	6	Year 2 – Chapter 8
Know and use halving as the inverse of doubling	5, 6	Year 2 – Chapter 8
Know by heart multiplication facts for the 2 and 10 times tables (later 5)	6	Year 2 – Chapter 8
Use mental strategies to solve simple problems with money, using a range of methods and explaining reasoning orally	7	Year 2 – Chapters 2 and 9

Counting and number sequences

Overall learning objectives

■ Count, saying the number names in order up to 100.

■ Describe and extend simple number sequences; count on or back in 1's or 10's, starting from any two-digit number.

> **Key words**
>
> | | |
> |---|---|
> | count | next |
> | zero, one, two to twenty and beyond | more |
> | | less |
> | how many? | odd |
> | count on/back | even |

Counting

Assessment focus

■ Can the children accurately count forwards/backwards in 1's to 100 from any starting number, read the number names and reliably count objects to 10, 20, 100?

Resources

■ a large 100 square

■ digit cards and number name cards

■ a drum or tambourine

■ Resource sheets 1, 2, 3, 4 and 5

■ small items, such as cubes, in bags for counting

■ dominoes

■ spinners or dice

■ large number cards and number names

With the whole class

■ Count forward and back to 20, 50 and 100 until all the children can recite the numbers to 100 accurately. Give extra practice in odd moments, such as when lining up for assembly. Give small groups tasks such as "Count from 5 to 25 and then back again," so that you can observe progress.

■ Stand the children in a circle, and distribute large number cards randomly among them. Display a large 100 square and then lay cards out in the centre of the circle to make a large 100 square. Repeat the process, laying matching number names on top of the digit cards, for example 'two' on top of '2'.

■ Hold up large domino/dice dot patterns (Resource sheets 3 and 4) so that the children can visualise these numbers and tell you the number immediately.

■ Beat a drum or tambourine and ask the children to count along. Make this progressively harder by holding the drum out of sight of the children, or by using an irregular beat.

■ Write multiples of 10 up to 100 on the board. Then count around the class three times in 1's from 0 to 30, each child saying a number. Explain that if their number is a multiple of 10 they should jump up when they say it. Repeat this with 0 to 40, then to 50 and then to 100.

With the lower-achievers

With adult support

Choose from:

1 Repeat any of the whole-class activities, observing who needs more help with counting.

2 Ask each child individually to count out a specific number of cubes or other small items. Observe who achieves one-to-one correspondence, even when numbers go beyond 10. Give those children number cards to suit their experience, such as 19 and 25, and ask them to count out objects to match. While they do that, you can work with those still struggling with numbers up to 10.

3 With prepared bags of objects, demonstrate how to count by grouping objects in 10's. Assess children's accuracy in counting. Demonstrate how to check each group of 10. (It is important to use numbers beyond 20, even if the children are struggling with one-to-one correspondence.)

4 Demonstrate how to count in 2's, making groups of 10.

5 Demonstrate tallying in 5's, making one mark for each object. Group and count items in 5's and then show how to make groups of 10 by merging two groups.

Teacher-independent activities

Choose from:

1 Give out digit cards or number name cards and ask the children to count out objects in relation to the numbers on the cards. These should be checked later by you or by a reliable child.

2 Using small items in bags as in activity 3 on the previous page, let the children count the items and match them to a digit card.

3 Invite the children to take large handfuls of cubes, count them in 2's and then group them in 10's to find out how many there are.

4 Playing dominoes can help to establish mental images of numbers to 6.

5 Make cards using Resource sheets 1 to 4 and give them to small groups. Invite them to match the digit cards to the domino patterns. Extend this eventually to matching the cards to the correct word cards.

6 Fill in Resource sheet 5 with numbers your children need to learn to recognise. Let them take turns to use a spinner or dice to generate numbers and then cover those numbers on their sheet with cubes. The first to cover all their numbers is the winner.

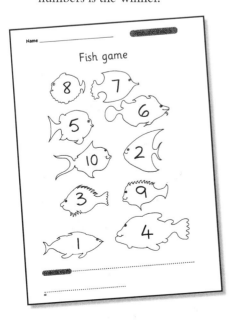

Plenary session

- *"Who would like to count to 20, 50, 100, with a friend?"*

- *"Let's all count back from 96 and stop at 20."*

- *"How many cubes did you have in your big handful? How did you check it? Let's check it together. First count the 'trains' of 10 – 10, 20, 30, 40 – and 2, 3, 4 more makes how many altogether? Find that number on the 100 square."*

- Hold up domino and word cards again and challenge individuals to read them.

- *"Who would like more help with counting in 1's?"*

- *"Find the card that says the word 'twenty'."*

Number lines

Assessment focus

- Can the children count on 1 and count back 1 from any starting number?

Resources

- a large number line or 100 square and floor number track to 20

- 1–9 dice or spinners

- 'count on 1/count on 2' spinners

- counters or cubes

- small 'add 1' and 'subtract 1' cards (eg 4 + 1 =)

- Resource sheets 1, 2, 5, 6, 7, 8 and 69

With the whole class

- Tell the children that today you will be looking at counting on and back in 1's. Display a large number line and point along it as they count forward and back. Try counting in 1's, starting at a number other than 0. Explain that to count on 1 means to count the next number.

- Write a number on the board and say that this is the starter number. Invite a child to find it on the number line or square. Tell the children to listen to the number of times you clap and count on that amount in their head. For example, if your starter number is 36 and you clap 7 times, the children count on in their heads 37, 38, 39, 40, 41, 42, 43. What number they have reached? Repeat the process, letting individual children do the clapping. Repeat with counting back. Explain that to count back 1 means to count the number before.

■ Finally write up two numbers below 100, such as 24 and 56. Challenge the children to count on in 1's from the first to the second. Repeat this with other numbers, counting on and counting back.

With the lower-achievers

With adult support

Choose from:

1   Let the children count along a floor number track to 20. Observe who takes one step for each number word. (For any children who need more help with counting, use the *Reception* or *Year 1* books in this series.) Give instructions, such as *"Stand on 5, and count on 1 more. What number are you on now? What if you count back 1?"*

2   Give each child a pile of cubes or counters. Give instructions, such as *"Count out 6 cubes. If you add 1 more, how many will you have?"* Observe who can add on 1 accurately. Repeat with taking 1 cube away.

3   Give each child a copy of Resource sheet 6. Work together to write 0 on the start. Ask *"What is 1 more than 0?"* Help them to write 1 in the next space. Ask different children to count on 1 more each time and then write in the next number together. Observe who writes numbers confidently and accurately. Keep the completed tracks for use in addition and subtraction.

4   Play 'Add 1 Lotto'. Use half of Resource sheet 7 to make a 'Lotto' board with numbers written in to suit your children, for example between 1 and 20. Give each child a 'Lotto/Bingo' board. Let them take turns to turn over a number card (Resource sheets 1 and 2) and read out the number. They then have to count on 1 from that number. If any of the children have the resulting number on their board, they can cover it with a counter. Alternatively, you could use 'add 1' cards, such as 4 + 1 =. The first player to cover all their numbers is the winner.

5   Play 'Subtract 1 Lotto' in the same way, but counting back 1 each time. Alternatively, you could use 'subtract 1' cards, such as 7 – 1 =.

6   Write 6 + 1 = on the board. Point to a 6 on the number track (Resource sheet 6) and say *"Add on 1 equals 7,"* demonstrating how to jump on 1 and where to write the 7 on the board. Stress that adding 1 means the next number. Repeat this with all numbers up to 9. Later on, repeat the process with subtract 1. When the children are ready, repeat this for count on 2 and 3.

7   See also Chapter 2 for adding 1 and 10.

Teacher-independent activities

Choose from:

1   Let the children work in pairs using a 'count on 1'/'count on 2' spinner (see page 4). Ask them to use their number tracks from Resource sheet 6 and take turns to spin the spinner and race to the end of the track.

2   Fill in the first space of each line on Resource sheet 8 with numbers such as 2, 4, 1 and 3. Tell the children that they have to count on 1 each time and so fill in each row. (Make sure there is a large number line or 100 square on display.) As they become more confident, you can change the picture at the top of the sheet, choosing one from the clip art on Resource sheet 69, and give more challenging starting numbers, such as 13, 27 and 35.

3   Let the children work in pairs to play the fish game on a blank copy of Resource sheet 5. Tell them to take turns to throw a 1–9 dice (or use a spinner), add 1 to whatever they throw and write the answer on one of the fish. When they have filled in all the fish, they should continue throwing and adding 1 but then cross out the numbers as they get them. The first to cross out all their fish numbers wins. On another day, play the game by counting back 1 each time.

4   Provide sets of 'add 1' cards, such as 5 + 1 =. Let the children work in pairs, putting a number card with the correct answer next to the 'add 1' card. Repeat this using 'subtract 1' cards.

Plenary session

- Remind the children that when we add/count on 1, the answer is the next number. Ask them what 9 + 1, 12 + 1 and so on are.

- Remind the children that when we subtract/ count back 1, the answer is the number before. Ask what 7 – 1, 8 – 1 and so on are.

- Play the fish game on a large copy of Resource sheet 5 in two teams.

- *"What have you learned today?"*

Counting on in 10's

Assessment focus

- Can the children count in 10's to 100?

- Can they count in 10's from a number other than a multiple of 10?

Resources

- a large 0–20 and 0–100 number line and 100 square

- Resource sheets 1, 2, 5, 7, 8, 9, 10, 11 and 69

- 1–10 dice or spinners

- counters

- place value cards

- a 10-minute timer

- crayons

With the whole class

- Using a 0–20 number line, start at 1 and count on 10, drawing a large 'add 10' jump on the board.

```
        +10
      ⌒              1 + 10 = 11
  ┌────────┐
├─●────────●──────────────┤
0 1        10 11          20
```

- Write up 1 + 10 = 11. Repeat this for 2 + 10, 3 + 10 and so on. What do the children notice? Point out the pattern that emerges when you count on 10.

- On a large 100 square, show how the 'add 10' pattern appears when you go down a line on the square – 3, 13, 23, 33, 43 and so on. It is valuable to give experience with a 100 square with 1 at the bottom left and also to use a 0–99 square. (Use an enlarged copy of Resource sheet 10 for this.)

- Write a multiple of 10 on the board and ask the children how many 10's and 1's are in it. Discuss what the answer will be if you add another 10, for example *"40 has four 10's and no 1's. If I add another 10 the answer will be 50."* (Link this to the use of place value cards.) Repeat the process using other multiples of 10.

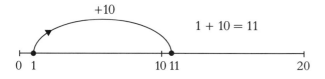

- Then do the same for numbers other than multiples of 10, stressing that the 1's come last. Tell them that they are going to count on in 10's. Using a 100 square, point to each number to maintain a steady pace. Stop while counting and ask individual children questions, such as *"7, 17, 27, 37, 47… What is 47 add 10?"* (Again, link this to the use of place value cards.)

- Make sure all the children can count in multiples of 10, both forwards and backwards, and can follow the pattern on a 100 square.

With the lower-achievers

With adult support

Choose from:

1   Fill in the fish on Resource sheet 5 with numbers 11 to 20. Give each child different coloured counters. They take turns to roll a 1–10 dice add 10 to the number thrown, for example 6 add 10 more equals 16, and then cover the correspondingly numbered fish with one of their counters. When all the fish are covered, the child with the most counters on the board wins. (This can be used as a teacher-independent activity once the children know it.)

2   Play 'Match the Cards'. Use Resource sheets 1 and 2 to make a set of 0–20 cards. Place the cards randomly face down and let the children take turns to turn over two cards. If the cards have a difference of 10, such as 6 and 16, the child can keep the pair. It not, the cards have to be put back in the same place. The child with the most pairs at the end of the game is the winner.

3   Shuffle a set of 1–10 cards. Ask the children to write down three numbers between 11 and 20. Hold up the top card and explain that if any of the children has 10 more than this in their list, they should cross it off. So if you hold up 6, the children can cross out 16. The first child to cross out all three of their numbers wins. Extend this to a 'Lotto/Bingo' game using half of Resource sheet 7 filled in with numbers 11 to 30.

4   Write 1 to 10 in a random list down one side of the board. Write the numbers 11 to 20 in a random list down the other side. Can the children match the 1 to 10 numbers with those that are 10 more? Repeat the process with two more random lists.

5   Using Resource sheet 10, work with the children to fill in the vertical rows by adding 10's onto a starting number. For example, starting in the top row with 5, write in 15, 25 and so on down the column until each column is filled in. (This can be developed into a game – see below.)

Teacher-independent activities

Choose from:

1   Using a copy each of Resource sheet 10 and a 1–10 dice or spinner, let pairs of children take turns to spin the spinner and put their number in the correct square in the top row. If their partner agrees that they have put it in the right place, the child can fill in all the other numbers in that column by adding on 10 each time. So if they throw a 5, they fill in numbers from 5 to 95. If a child places their starting number in the wrong position in the top row, they miss a go. The winner is the first player to fill in the whole square. (Have a 100 square on display for reference, or give each pair of children a copy of Resource sheet 9.)

2   Using Resource sheet 11, write starting numbers and the mapping operation 'Count on 10'. Let the children have a 100 square or number line for reference, and ask them to write in the answers. (Use a different picture from Resource sheet 69 to use this sheet again.)

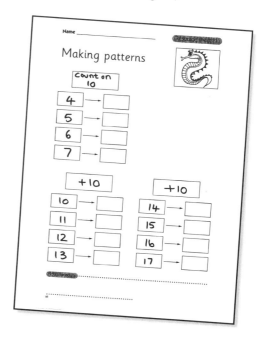

3   Those children that need the experience can work in pairs to practise chanting numbers down a vertical column on Resource sheet 9. Let them colour in the columns they know and demonstrate their chants at the plenary session.

4   Using Resource sheet 10 and a 10-minute timer, challenge children to fill in all the numbers from 1–100 before the timer rings.

5   Those that need more practice with counting on in 10's can use Resource sheet 8 filled in with starting numbers, and continue the sequence adding 10 each time.

Plenary session

■   *"What is 56 + 10? What is 10 more than 62? Chant in 10's from 7 for us. Come and point to the column I am counting in: 46, 56, 66, 76."*

■   *"I have drawn a number line on the board. Someone come and draw 5 add 10 on my number line."*

■   *"Who will chant back from 100 to 10 with a friend?"*

Counting back in 10's

Assessment focus

■ Can the children count back/subtract in 10's from 100 and from numbers other than multiples of 10?

Resources

■ a 0–20 number line, a 1–20 floor track and a 100 square

■ a timer

■ place value cards

■ 11–19 spinners

■ 'count on 10/count back 10' spinners and 'count back 10/count back 1' spinners

■ Resource sheets 1, 2, 5, 8, 10, 11, 12 and 13

■ cubes and small counters

With the whole class

■ Using a 0–20 line, start at 19 and count back 10. Demonstrate that as a jump back of 10.

![Number line showing a jump back of -10 from 19 to 9, marked at 0, 9 10, and 19 20]

■ Write 19 – 10 = 9 on the board. Repeat this for 18, 17 and 16. What do the children notice? Point out the pattern. Ask random questions, such as 14 – 10. Tell the class that they are going to try to beat the clock. Give each child in turn a question using teen numbers, such as 17 – 10. Time how long it takes them to say the answer. Repeat the questioning, challenging the children to try to beat their previous time.

■ Write up a multiple of 10, such as 50, and say *"This is my starting number. How many 10's and 1's are in it? If I take one 10 away, what will the answer be?"* Repeat the process with other numbers. Then write up a number other than a multiple

of 10 and ask how many 10's and 1's there are in it. Stress that the 1's come last. Demonstrate how to take one 10 away using place value cards, for example *"47 has four 10's and seven 1's. If I take one of the 10's away I am left with 37."*

■ Tell the children that they are going to count back in 10's using a 100 square. Point to the numbers, stopping to ask questions, such as *"98, 88, 78, 68… What is 68 subtract 10?"*

With the lower-achievers

With adult support

Choose from:

1 Write the numbers 1–9 on the fish on Resource sheet 5. (Repeat one number as there are 10 fish.) Give the children some counters, a different colour for each child. Let them take turns to spin an 11–19 spinner. Whatever number they get, they should subtract 10 from it, and cover the correspondingly numbered fish with one of their counters. The child with the most fish covered at the end of the game is the winner. (Once learned, this game can be teacher-independent.)

2 Using place value cards, work with children making numbers up to 100, first partitioning them into 10's and 1's, and leading into subtracting 10 from the numbers you make. Link this to counting backwards in 10's on a 100 square.

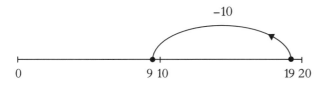

3 Using Resource sheet 10, ask the children to fill in one column at a time, starting from a number in the 90's and deducting 10 each time. So, starting at 96 they can fill in 86, 76 and so on. Make sure each child can count back in 10's from a number in the 90's.

4 Using Resource sheet 12 filled in as shown overleaf, show the children how to play a 'Three in a row' game, working in pairs with their own colour cubes. Invite them to start by choosing a square on the grid that they are aiming to cover, for example 9. They spin the spinner to find if they must count on or back 10. If they spin 'count back 10' and they want to cover square 9,

they must decide which number they need to choose as a starting number from the treasure chest (in this case they need to choose 19 to count back 10 to get an answer of 9). They should then cover 9 with one of their cubes. The winner is the first child to place three cubes in a row in any direction.

5   For a simpler game using Resource sheet 12, fill in the grid randomly with numbers from 1 to 10. Prepare 11–20 number cards from Resource sheets 1 and 2 and place them face down between two children. Invite them to take turns to turn over a number card, count back 10 from their number and cover the resulting number on the grid with one of their cubes or counters. The winner is the child with the most cubes or counters on the grid at the end of a given time.

Teacher-independent activities

Choose from:

1   Fill in starting numbers on Resource sheets 8 and 11 as before, but this time requiring children to count back 10 each time.

2   Play one of the games on Resource sheet 12 as described in activity 4 and 5 above.

3   Using a large floor number track (1–20), ask the children to choose a number to start on and then count back 10 steps.

4   Use Resource sheet 13 and a spinner (see page 4) to make a 'Count back 10/count back 1' game. Ask the children to place a small counter on 50, take turns to spin the spinner and then count back as appropriate. The winner is the first to get to the end of the snake. Extend the game by asking the children to record each of their turns in their own way. Vary the game by using a different spinner, for example counting back 1, 2, 3 or 4, as well as 10.

Plenary session

■   *"What is 15 subtract 10?"*

■   *"What is 10 less than 36?"*

■   *"Who can count back in 10's from 86?"*

■   *"What did you like best about maths today?"*

■   Play the 'Three in a Row' game (Resource sheet 12) in two teams.

Odd or even?

Assessment focus

■   Can the children recognise odd and even numbers up to 100?

Resources

■   a large 100 square

■   cubes, counters and 1–6 dice

■   green and red marker pens

■   green and red crayons

■   Resource sheets 1, 3, 4, 9, 13 and 67

■   a small bag

With the whole class

■   Give pairs of children 10 cubes. On the board, draw two columns headed 'odd' and 'even'. Tell the class that they are going to look at odd and even numbers. Explain that if a number can be shared equally between two then it is even, but if there is one left over it is odd. Choose a number, for example 8. Ask the pairs of children to share out the appropriate number of cubes and establish that the number is even. Write 8 in the 'Even' column.

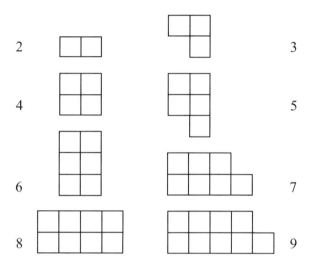

2, 4, 6 and 8 make pairs, but 3, 5, 7 and 9 have an odd one sticking out.

■ Start circling in green all the even numbers on a 100 square, saying the numbers out loud as you do so. Stop at 20 and ask *"What comes next?"* Ask how many you are counting on each time. Continue counting and circling numbers up to 100, stopping occasionally to ask what number comes next. Ask the children if they can see a pattern and if they can tell you anything about even numbers. Tell them that all even numbers end in 0, 2, 4, 6 or 8.

■ Repeat the process with odd numbers, circling them in red. Tell the class that you can tell if a number is odd or even by looking at how many 1's it has, for example *"62 ends in two 1's: therefore it is even."* Ask individual children whether numbers are odd or even and why.

■ Count to 100, saying all the odd numbers in a quiet voice and all the even numbers in a silly voice (if you can stand it!).

■ During PE, choose one side of the hall to be 'odd' and the other to be 'even'. Ask one child to call out a number between 1 and 100. The other children must run to the correct side of the hall.

With the lower-achievers

With adult support

Choose from:

1 Repeat sharing out cubes into pairs as in the whole-class activity. Make sure each child understands about putting cubes in pairs. (As you are doing this, assess the counting skills of individual children who have needed extra help with counting.)

2 Write a few numbers on the board and then ask the children to say which ones are odd and which are even. Try to move them on to looking at the endings of numbers and making generalised statements about even and odd numbers, such as *"All even numbers end in 0, 2, 4 6 or 8."*

3 Use Resource sheet 1 to make the number cards from 1 to 10. Place them in a bag, and let the children take turns to pull out a number and call it out. The first child to shout *"Odd"* or *"Even"* correctly wins a cube. The winner is the child with the most cubes at the end of a given time – but only if they can tell you whether their number of cubes is odd or even!

Teacher-independent activities

Choose from:

1 Give each child a 100 square (Resource sheet 9) and ask them to circle all the even numbers in green and the odd numbers in red. Ask them to think about any patterns they notice.

2 Give pairs of children 20 cubes. Ask them to sort all the numbers from 1 to 20 into odd or even, and record their findings.

3 Give pairs of children copies of Resource sheet 13. Ask them to place a counter on the snake's head and then take turns to throw a 1–6 dice to find how many spaces they must count back. Explain that when they land on a number, they must decide together if it is odd or even. Ask them to colour even numbers in green and odd numbers in red for sharing later in the plenary session.

4 Give children the cards from Resource sheets 3 and 4 and ask them to sort them into odd and even numbers.

Chapter 1

5   Make a sheet using cut-outs from Resource
    sheet 67. The children have to count the objects
    and write the number in green if it is even and
    red if it is odd.

Plenary session

- *"Tell me all the even numbers up to 10."*

- *"Is 43 odd or even? How do you know?"*

- *"Who can tell me how you can recognise an even
  number?"* (You are aiming at the children looking
  at the ending of the number.)

- *"Would 49/76/100/101 be an odd or an even
  number? How could you find out?"*

- *"Tell us about the pattern of reds and greens you made
  on your 100 square."*

- For more on number sequences, see Chapter 6.

Ordering and place value

Overall learning objectives

- Know what each digit represents, including 0 as a place holder, with numbers up to 100.

- Read, write and order whole numbers up to 100.

- Understand the language of comparing and ordering.

Key words

same number as	least
as many as	compare
more	order
larger/largest	before
fewer/fewest	after
smaller/smallest	between

Greater/less than

Assessment focus

- Can the children compare numbers using 'greater than'/'less than', 'fewer than'/'more than', with numbers to 100 (and say a number that is 1 more and 10 more)?

Resources

- a 0–20 number line
- cubes, two 1–9 dice and two 1–6 dice
- Resource sheets 1, 2, 3, 4, 11, 14, 15 and 67
- a washing line, pegs and large number cards to 100
- word cards: 'is greater than', 'is less than', 'is fewer than' and so on
- Blu-tack
- a small bag
- place value cards

With the whole class

- Ask the children to choose two number cards under 20, such as 14 and 8. Ask which number is the greater. Invite them to put the number cards on the washing line so that the larger of the two numbers is to the right. Repeat this with two more numbers, putting the cards at about the right place on the washing line. Establish that the lower number is to the left and the larger to the right. *"Think of a number that would be even further to the right than 14. Would 10 go to the left or the right of 8?"* Many children have problems with left and right, so ask them to point to the end of the line that has the greater numbers. *"This number is 18. Point to the side it will go on. So it is to the right of 17."*

- Repeat the washing line activity with numbers 10 to 30. Establish that as we count forward, the numbers get larger and larger. If we count to 30, that is the largest number in that count. If we count to 100, the last number we say is 100, so that is the largest number in that count.

- Draw two columns on the board, one labelled '10 or greater than 10' and the other '10 or less than 10'. Split the class into two teams, one 'greater than' and the other 'less than'. Let the children take turns to throw two 1–9 dice and add the scores. If the total is 10, both teams score a point. If it is less than 10, the 'less than' team scores a point; if it is greater than 10, the other team gets a point.

- In a space where noise doesn't matter, give out the number cards 1 to 30, one per child, and ask the class to put themselves in order. Repeat the activity in small groups, giving out a selection of numbers (not a complete set) and asking them to order their set. Invite the children to go around the groups once all the cards are in place so they can check everyone is right. Emphasise the language, for example *"87 goes to the right of 56 because 87 is more than 56."*

With the lower-achievers

With adult support

Choose from:

1   Use cubes to make two towers, one of 5 cubes and one of 10. Put them side by side. Ask *"Which has the most cubes?"* Talk about 10 being

'more than'/'greater than' 5. Point to 10 and 5 on the number line and show how 10 is to the right of 5. Explain that 10 is worth more than 5. Repeat the process with other towers of cubes. Let the children make their own towers and tell you which is 'greater than' the other and therefore worth more. Write the statements on the board, using Blu-tack to stick up 'is greater than' and 'is less than' cards.

2   Use Resource sheets 1 and 2 to make a set of 0–20 number cards. Give two cards to a child and ask her to tell you which is the greater, using cubes or a number line if necessary. Repeat this with other children.

3   Let the children take turns to throw two 1–6 dice and decide which number is the greater.

4   Use Resource sheets 1 and 2 to make two sets of 0–20 cards. Shuffle both sets and put them face down in their separate piles. Let the children take turns to turn over the top card from each pile. Give them the 'is greater than' and 'is less than' word cards and ask them to choose the correct one to put between the two numbers. Encourage them to use the correct language, for example '6 is less than 10'.

5   Make links to the work done in Chapter 1 by asking for numbers 1 more (or less) and 10 more (or less). This can be recorded on Resource sheet 11.

Teacher-independent activities

Choose from:

1   Use two sets of 0–20 cards with the two 10's removed. On a large sheet of paper draw two columns headed 'less than 10' and 'greater than 10'. Shuffle and mix the cards together. Let the children turn over the cards, decide if the number is greater than or less than 10 and write it in the correct column. Explain that the whole class will discuss this in the plenary session.

2   Let the children use Resource sheet 14. Numbers can be suggested by you or generated by the children taking two cards out of a bag.

3   The children could work in pairs to complete Resource sheet 15, circling the larger of two numbers. If your children need additional experience of this kind of activity, cut out small pictures from the clip art on Resource sheet 67 to make more sheets.

4   Use Resource sheets 3 and 4 to make cards. Let a pair of children each pick up a card from a face down pack and decide who has the larger number. That player wins both the cards. The winner is the player with the most cards at the end.

Plenary session

■   *"Which is the greater number, 6 or 24?"*

■   *"Which is less, 90 or 50?"*

■   *"Is 4 fewer than or more than 3?"*

■   Using place value cards in preparation for later work, compare 2 two-digit numbers and decide which is greater by looking at the 10's and the 1's.

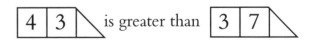

■   Look at the chart that the children working independently made showing numbers less than 10 and greater than 10. Do the others in the class agree with their decisions?

Ordering

Assessment focus

- Can the children order numbers to 10, 20, 50, 100 (and say a number that lies between)?

Resources

- a washing line and large number cards
- a number line
- place value cards
- Resource sheets 1, 2, 3, 4, 6 and 8
- 1–6 dice

With the whole class

- Order number cards on a washing line or with the children holding them up. Ask the children to say why one number comes before another by looking at the 10's digit and the units. Go over the fact that larger numbers are to the right on the number line.

- Ask the children to work in small groups to order complete sets of numbers according to their experience. Develop this to ordering just a selection of numbers.

- Display numbers to 10 or 20 on a washing line. Ask the children to close their eyes while you turn round or swap some numbers. Invite some of the lower-achievers to tell you the numbers that have been turned round or swapped.

- Use the washing line to talk about numbers in between, for example *"Dan, give me a number that comes in between 14 and 19."*

- Ask the children to use place value cards to make the number just before 15, 10 more than 24, the number with one 10 and five units, the number just after 19 and so on.

With the lower-achievers

With adult support

Choose from:

1   Go over the activities from the whole-class session, making sure all the children are confident with using place value cards and can say why a number is greater than or fewer than another number.

2   Make sure all the children can order cards to 10 and then to 20 on their own. Repeat this until they are confident.

3   Ask the children for numbers that go in between two other numbers and for numbers 1 more and 10 more than a given number.

Teacher-independent activities

Choose from:

1   Let the children work in pairs to order sets of number cards made from Resource sheets 1 and 2, both complete sets and incomplete sets. They need a large table so that they can leave the cards out for you to check. Include some ordering backwards, such as starting at 20 and going back to 0. (Any children still struggling to order cards to 10 and 20 will need to do this every day until they are confident.)

2   Use the dotted cards from Resource sheets 3 and 4 for the children to order.

3   Fill in Resource sheet 8 so that the children can put in the missing numbers.

4 Children who need more help can write numbers in the spaces on Resource sheet 6 and then use the sheet to play a race game using a 1–6 dice. If the children are struggling with writing and ordering numbers to 20 and above, give them intensive help with this every day for a while.

Plenary session

■ Go over the children's ordered cards with the whole class, counting as you do so.

■ Count forwards and backwards to 10, 20, 100.

■ *"Which number comes just before 20? Is 19 before or after 21 when we count forwards?"*

■ *"Who would like to take a set of cards home to practise ordering them?"*

■ Divide the class into two equal teams and give each child a number card. Ask the teams to race to order themselves according to their number cards.

10's and 1's

Assessment focus

■ Can the children say what a digit represents in a two-digit number and partition numbers into 10's and 1's?

Resources

■ Resource sheets 9 and 16

■ Dienes equipment and abacuses

■ a PE hoop, three ice cream boxes and beanbags

■ a large 100 square and number line to 100

■ place value cards

■ large coins (such as Mega Money from BEAM)

With the whole class

■ Tell the class that today you will be looking at tens and units. Remind them that the 1's always come last. Using a large 100 square, ask individual children to find different numbers,

for example a number with four 10's and six 1's (46), a number with the same amount of 10's and 1's (77) and all the numbers that end in three 1's (13, 23, 33 and so on). Establish that with the last example there is a pattern – the whole column ends in the same number. Say *"Now we're going to play 'Find the number'. I'm thinking of a number,"* (for example 22) *"and you can have six questions and three guesses to find it."* Demonstrate good questions to ask, for example *"Is it greater than 50?"* (Cross out all the numbers on the 100 square from 51 to 100.) *"Is it odd?"* (Cross out all the numbers that end in 1, 3, 5, 7 or 9.) *"Has it got six 1's?"* (Cross out all the numbers ending in 6.) *"Has it got three 10's?"* (Cross out all the 30 numbers.) When they have asked six questions, let the children have three guesses at what the number is. Play again, letting individual children think of the number.

■ Play a throwing game. Ask the children to form a circle around a PE hoop with three ice cream containers inside it. Ask one child to throw six beanbags into the hoop. Explain that if the beanbags land in the hoop they are 1's, and if they land in the containers they count as 10's. The children should each count up their score, starting with the 10's, and write it on the board, explaining the process as they do so. For example, *"One 10 and five 1's – that's 15."* Repeat the process until everyone has had a turn.

■ Let the children lay out their place value cards on the table in front of them. Call out a number for them to make, such as 24, 78 and 92. Each time establish how many 10's and how many 1's there are. Find each number on the 100 square. Recap on which number is greater if necessary. You can also ask individuals to make the numbers on an abacus, with Dienes apparatus or with 10p and 1p pieces, and find them on a number line.

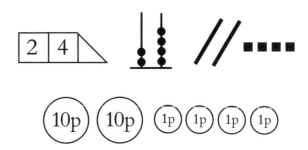

With the lower-achievers

With adult support

Choose from:

1 Use Dienes apparatus to display some numbers under 10. Ask the children to use place value cards to show what numbers they represent. For example, if you make 8, write 8 on the board and ask the children to make 8 with their place value cards. Then put out ten 1's and exchange them for one 10, explaining that ten 1's are worth one 10. (Relate this to coins, either now or in another lesson.) Put out a number above 10, such as 14, and count on from 10 – *"11, 12, 13, 14."* Write the numbers on the board, telling the children that the 1's always come last in a number. Again, invite them to make the number with their place value cards. Repeat the process for other numbers under 100. Then let them take turns writing out the numbers, each time reminding them that the 1's come last.

2 Give pairs of children a 100 square (Resource sheet 9), and let them take turns to play the 'Find the number' game as described in the whole-class starter activities.

3 Invite the children to choose a number from a large 100 square and make it using place value cards. Then split the numbers, for example *"45 splits into four 10's and five 1's."* Emphasise the teen numbers as well as numbers above 20 so that children can see the pattern of numbers beyond 20. Reverse the activity by saying the split number first and then asking the children to say what the number is, for example *"My number is seven 10's and two 1's. What is it?"*

4 Give further experience with saying what is 1 more/less and what is 10 more/less than a number.

Teacher-independent activities

Choose from:

1 Let the children play the throwing game described in the whole-class starter activities in groups. Write their names at the top of individual columns on a chart. Ask them to take turns to throw the beanbags as before and write up their score in their column. The player with the highest score in each round wins 10 points.

Ask them to take the scores to the plenary session to talk about the numbers.

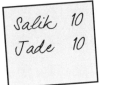

| Salik | 10 |
| Jade | 10 |

Jade	Salik	Ceris
13	21	4
14	3	11

2 Provide children with place value cards and a filled-in version of Resource sheet 16. Ask them to make the number with the cards and then split it to complete the sheet.

3 Use the sheet again with other numbers.

Plenary session

- *"How many 1's in 26?"*

- *"How many 10's in 75?"*

- *"What is 10 more than 19?"*

- *"When I split my number it is four 10's and nine 1's. What is one more than my number?"*

- Look at the scores the children working independently achieved in the throwing game.

- *"What you have been learning about today is very important and will help you with adding and subtracting."* (It is important that children are able to partition numbers up to 100 and beyond in order to underpin their work on calculating.)

Addition

Overall learning objectives

- Know by heart all pairs of numbers with a total of 10/20.

- Understand addition as counting on and use the symbols '+' and '='.

- Understand that addition can be done in any order and start to use a range of strategies for addition.

> ### Key words
>
> | | |
> |---|---|
> | and | equals |
> | add | altogether |
> | plus | more |
> | total | partner |

Fingers

Assessment focus

- Do the children know the addition number facts for a given number bond?

Resources

- Unifix cubes
- Resource sheets 1, 5, 6, 17, 18, 19 and 20
- large number cards and a class number line
- sticky notes
- coloured felt-tipped pens
- 1–6 dice
- spinner with numbers up to the bond being worked on
- timer or stopwatch

With the whole class

- Play 'Fingers'. Ask the children to hold up 10 fingers. Then tell them how many to fold down, asking for the number bond, for example *"2 down, so 8 are left standing up, 2 + 8 = 10."*

- Play 'Ping Pong' to 10. Explain that you are going to say a number, for example 7, and they must reply with the number that makes it up to 10 (3). However, if you say *"Ping"* the class has to say *"Pong"*. The 'Ping' and 'Pong' will help you to maintain a good pace. Over the weeks repeat the game and gradually build up speed, checking that all the children are joining in.

- Later, when bonds to 10 are established, give pairs of children 20 Unifix cubes joined in 'trains' of 10's. Say *"Today we are going to work on our number bonds to 20 and learn the number partners by heart. Using only one train of 10, take one cube off and tell your partner the number bond."* Write 1 + 9 = 10 on the board. Repeat the process until you have all the number bonds.

- Say *"Now use both 10 'trains'. If 1 + 9 = 10, what do we add to 1 to make 20?"* Tell them to work it out using the cubes. Write 1 + 19 = 20 under 1 + 9 = 10. Ask them for other number 'partners' to 20 and repeat this until you have all the number bonds. *"Can you see a pattern? Look how knowing the number bonds to 10 helps us know the number facts to 20."*

- Work on other number bonds, for example making a 'train' of 8 and splitting this up systematically (7 + 1 and 6 + 2).

With the lower-achievers

With adult support

Choose from:

1   Work on number bonds below 10, such as 8. Hold up a large number card 8 and ask the children to hold up 8 fingers. Explain that you will be working with 8 this lesson. Ask the children to fold down 3 fingers. *"How many are left? So the number 'partner' for 3 is 5 when we are working with 8."* Then choose a child to say the number fact, for example *"3 add 5 is 8."* Repeat this for other facts to 8.

2   Play 'Number Partners for 8'. Using the cards 0 to 8 (either large cards for a big group or use Resource sheet 1), write the 'partner' number on the back of each one in a different colour. For example, on the back of a black 2 you write a red 6. Demonstrate how to count on to find the number to put on the back. Practise and then play it as a game, turning the card over to

check. The child who calls out the correct partner the quickest wins that card. The child with the most cards at the end wins the game.

3   Mark 8 on the class number line with a sticky note. Say *"We are going to find 3's partner for 8. Start on 3 and count on to 8. So the partner is the difference between the two numbers. So from 3 we count on 4, 5, 6, 7, 8, which is 5 jumps. Therefore 3 and 5 equals 8."* Let the children take turns to write each sum as they work it out.

4   Play a game in pairs, using the number partners for 8, 10 and so on. Use Resource sheet 5 for each child and a 1–6 dice. Let the children take turns throwing the dice and writing that number's partner to make 8 on a fish. So if 6 is thrown, they should write 2 on a fish. Let them use the number line or count on their fingers to find the partner. When they have filled in all the fish, they should continue to play, but this time cross out the partners. The first to cross all of them out is the winner. (Once the children have done this with you, it can be used as an independent activity with children working in pairs.) Develop the game using spinners up to the number bond you are working with, so a spinner for 10 would be 0–10.

Teacher-independent activities

Choose from:

1   Let the children play 'Find It' in pairs or small groups with a set of partner cards as prepared for the second adult-supported activity, for example cards that add up to 8 (7 has 1 on the back and so on). Ask them to spread the cards out and take turns to find a number. For example, if one child challenges another to find 6, the second child must turn over a 2 to find 6 on the other side. If she is right she wins a cube. The winner is the player who has the most cubes at the end. (It can help to stick to just one number bond in each lesson, so number bonds to 10 need a whole lesson and so on.)

2   Play 'Pelmanism' with two sets (or four sets to make a longer game) of 0–10 cards (or just 0–8 if appropriate). The children place the cards face down on the table and then take it in turns to find two cards that add up to 10 (or 8). If they are wrong, both cards have to be turned back in

exactly the same space. Pairs that are found can be kept. The winner is the player who has the most pairs at the end.

3   A follow-up to number bonds to 10 is on Resource sheet 17. Give the children 'trains' of 10 Unifix cubes and ask them to draw systematically what they find out. Show them how to draw cubes quickly. There isn't space on the sheet to draw around cubes but you could let them do that on a larger sheet.

4   Resource sheet 18 can be used to record other number bonds by splitting up cube 'trains'. Remember to make the link from bonds to 10 to bonds to 20.

5   Resource sheet 19 can be filled in to find pairs that make 10. (There will be some repeats.)

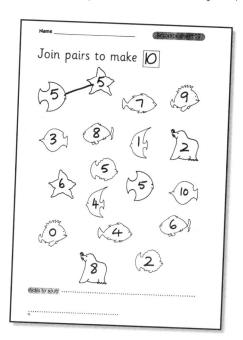

6   Use Resource sheet 19 again to repeat the activity with another number.

7   Using Resource sheet 20, give children a number, for example 10, and ask them to draw enough of each item to make 10 altogether.

Plenary session

- *"Tell me a pair of number partners for 8."*

- *"Think of 8 on a number line. How many hops back would I make to get to 5?"*

- *"If we know 1 add 9 is 10, tell me what we have to add to 1 to make 20."*

- Play a game of 'Number Partners to 10' on an enlarged version of Resource sheet 6 filled in as shown below. Divide the class into two teams. Let the teams take turns at looking at the next number on the track and calling out the number partner to make 10. So Team 1 must call out 7 to go with the 3. Then Team 2 must call out 5 to go with the 5, and so on. As a variation, when you are also working on time, set the timer and work just with one team, pointing to the numbers in turn and getting the children to call out the partner number as quickly as they can. The second team must then try to do it more quickly.

Adding

Assessment focus

- Can the children add two numbers under 20 using a number line or track?

Resources

- a floor number track

- cubes and small toys, such as teddies

- Resource sheets 1, 2, 3, 4, 5, 6, 11, 21, 22, 23, 24, 25 and 67

- small cards that read 'count on 1, 2, 3, 4' and so on

- counters and two 1–6 dice

- calculators

- a small bag

- scissors, glue and workbooks

With the whole class

- Use a large floor number track (numbers on scrap paper laid out across the floor are fine). Choose children to stand on a number and count on (or back), for example *"Stand on 3, count on 2 and you land on 5."* Repeat the process.

- Encourage the children to visualise the number track by closing their eyes. Then tell them to imagine standing on 8 and taking 1 step, and so on. This is a vital part of mental maths, so spend time visualising with everyone.

- Give each child or pair of children a number line or track, such as the one on Resource sheet 21. (You can make several lines just to 10 and use the 'blanks' to make others up to and beyond 20. Laminate these as they will be used extensively. Many children seem to make the link from a number track to a number line quite easily, but this line/track will help those who find the change harder.) Show the children how to use fingers to take 'steps' along the track, or give them small toys such as teddies that they can make 'jump' along the track. Say, for example, *"Stand on 4 and take 2 steps. Where are you now?"* Make sure that they take a step for each number they count. Follow this up when they play track games such as 'Ludo' or games using the track in this book.

- On the board, show the children how to draw steps along the line (see Resource sheet 22). Use a range of number lines and tracks to demonstrate this to help them to make the link between number tracks and number lines.

With the lower-achievers

With adult support

Choose from:

1   Use a 1–20 or 1–30 number line, depending on the children's needs. (Enlarge Resource sheet 21 or write numbers up to 28 on Resource sheet 6.) Have some small cards that say 'count on 1, 2, 3, 4' and so on. Let each child put a counter on the start and take turns to take a card and move their counter the correct number of steps. Watch carefully to make sure they do actually move one at the start of their count – lots of children count 'one' without moving on one space. The first child to reach the end wins. If they are having difficulty taking steps, go back to using the large floor number track or use fingers to take steps.

2   Give each child a piece of paper and ask them to write down three numbers between 2 and 12. Let them take turns to throw two 1–6 dice, say the sum, for example *"2, count on 5,"* and use their number line or track to take steps to find the answer (2 add 5 is 7). Any child with 7 written on their piece of paper can cross it off. The first child to have all three numbers crossed out is the winner.

3   On Resource sheet 21, show the children how to draw in steps along the line so that they will be able to complete Resource sheet 22.

4   Give each pair a copy of Resource sheet 5 filled in with numbers that can be made by adding the numbers thrown on two 1–6 dice (the numbers 2 to 12). Let them take turns to throw the dice and do the counting on along a floor number track or with fingers on a desk number track. When the answer is found, they cross off that number or cover the fish with a cube.

5   Make sure all the children can identify the '+' and '=' signs. An ideal way to do this is to give each child a calculator and ask them to enter 2 + 2 =. Give them time to explore the calculators as this can be an important part of learning to recognise symbols.

Teacher-independent activities

Choose from:

1   Use Resource sheet 11 to make some counting on tasks. Choose a simple operation, such as 'count on 2', for the top box. Fill in the starting numbers yourself or let the children throw the dice to get the starter number and write in the answer – '4 count on 2 is 6'.

2   Resource sheets 22 and 23 give further experience in counting on. Either choose the numbers for Resource sheet 23 yourself, or let the children choose them.

3   Resource sheet 25 is for children who need more practice counting on with objects as well as along a number line. You can make more sheets like this using the clip art from Resource sheet 67, but it is crucial to give the children more practical experience so use objects to count, as well as the pictures.

Addition needs to be understood as the combination of two or more sets of objects as well as counting on a number line.

4   Resource sheet 24 gives further practice and needs to be used with a number track. You could fill in the starting numbers and just add 1 each time if necessary, or let the children pick number cards (from Resource sheets 1 and 2) out of a bag.

5   The boxes of dots on Resource sheets 3 and 4 can be cut up by the children and stuck into workbooks, adding two of the sets, or simply counting and adding 1 more to each set each time.

Plenary session

- *"What is 8 add 2?"*
- *"What is 3 more than 7?"*
- *"Gerry, stand on 8 and count on 3. Who knows where he will land?"*
- *"Shut your eyes and imagine you are standing on a number line. Stand on number 5. Take 2 steps forward. Where are you?"*
- *"I took 4 steps and I landed on 5. What number did I start on?"*

Change it around

Assessment focus

- Can the children understand that addition can be done in any order?

Resources

- dice and spinners
- large number cards and a number line
- cubes
- coloured pens or crayons
- Resource sheets 1, 2, 12, 19, 26, 27 and 68
- Blu-tack and board

With the whole class

- Play 'Two Hand Wizz'. Invite two children to come to the front. Explain that on the count of 3 they must show one hand, each holding up a random number of fingers. For example, one child might hold up 3 fingers and the other might hold up 4. Help the class to add the two numbers (don't count from 1 each time!) by saying, *"Let's put the larger number in our heads and count on the 3."* Then establish that you would get the same answer if you had started with the 3 and then counted on 4. Repeat the game a few times. (Develop the game into larger numbers by playing 'Four Hand Wizz' where the children hold up fingers on both hands.)

- Repeat the activity by throwing two large dice and calling out the numbers. Establish that addition can be done in any order.

- Using large number cards, model putting the larger number first and then counting on. Have one set of 11–16 cards (or numbers to suit your children) and another set of 1–4. Let a child select one of the lower cards and another child take a higher number card.

"Let's swap these around and put the 12 first. Put 12 in your head and then count on 2."

- Extend this lesson on another day to changing the order of adding by finding a pair of numbers that make 10. For example, to add 6 and 3 and 4, add the 6 and the 4 to make 10 and then add 3 more. Show how to do this with large number cards, asking children to the front to pair the two numbers that make 10.

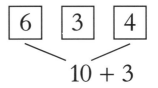

With the lower-achievers

With adult support

Choose from:

1. Repeat the introductory activities. Let the children physically swap around two number cards so that they are quite clear that the larger one must come first. (Make sure they can tell you which number is larger! See Chapter 2.) Observe all the children individually, checking

that they can hold the first number in their head and count on. (Use number lines or fingers and explain that if you are adding numbers such as 15 you don't want to do that with cubes! It would be far too slow!)

2   As a group, work on Resource sheet 26 and show how the curly arrow means to swap the numbers around. Generate numbers with number cards and/or dice.

3   When you are working on finding pairs to make 10, again use number cards, but give more experience with number bonds to 10 by asking the children to help you to write up 9 + 1, 8 + 2 and so on. You could use Resource sheet 19 for this. Show them how to put the two numbers that make 10 together, as on Resource sheet 27. You will probably need to work through this sheet with the children, maybe circling in colour the pair that makes 10 first.

Teacher-independent activities

Choose from:

1   Fill in a copy of Resource sheet 12 as shown below. Give the children coloured cubes (a different colour for each child). They take turns to spin the spinner and then choose a number from the treasure chest to add to the number they spun to make a number on the grid. They can then cover that number with a cube. The idea is to have three of their cubes in a row in any direction, and the first child to achieve this

is the winner. Emphasise that you want them to keep the spinner number in their head and then count on along a number line or on their fingers.

2   Give the children number cards (Resource sheets 1 and 2) and some Blu-tack. Ask them to work together to make sums with larger and smaller numbers, putting the larger one first. They should stick the cards to a board with Blu-tack. Tell them to be prepared to talk about what they have done in the plenary session. Say that they can work out the answers and write them down on another piece of paper.

3   To give more experience with finding pairs to make 10, price the items on Resource sheet 68 at 9p and 1p, 8p and 2p, and so on. Ask the children to pair up items that can be bought with exactly 10 pence.

Plenary session

■ *"What did you learn today?"*

■ *"Does it matter which order you add numbers in? Is 6 + 4 the same as 4 + 6? Why is it quicker to put the larger number in your head? Why do we find pairs to make 10?"* (To make adding quicker.)

Patterns

Assessment focus

■ Can the children add a single-digit number to multiples of 10 and see simple number patterns?

Resources

■ Resource sheets 5, 10, 11, 12 and 24

■ a large number line and 100 square

■ place value cards and an abacus

■ calculators

■ a 1–6 dice and a spinner marked in multiples of 10

■ cubes, coins, Blu-tack

With the whole class

■ Use place value cards to make multiples of 10 and then add a single-digit number. Make number patterns and chant them, for example *"40 add 4 is 44, 50 add 4 is 54,"* and so on.

30 add 4 makes 34.

■ Demonstrate the patterns on both a large 100 square and a number line. (Although a 100 square is useful to demonstrate the pattern, it is better for the children to use number lines to do calculations like this because they tend to get

lost on a 100 square after the multiple of 10, and sometimes count along the wrong line. A 0 to 99 square made using Resource sheet 10 will get around this problem as the multiple of 10 will always be at the start of the line.)

With the lower-achievers

With adult support

Choose from:

1 Using place value cards, put together a multiple of 10 and some 1's, such as 30 and 7, partition it again and set it out as a calculation with a '+' and '=' sign. Let the children explore the calculations on calculators. Set up a pattern of calculations with some extra 7 cards.

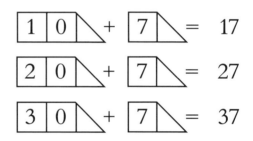

2 Provide a spinner marked 10, 20, 30 and 40 (see page 4) and a 1–6 dice. Let the children take turns to spin and throw the dice and say the number they have made. For example, a spin of 40 and a 5 on the dice would make 45. (Extend the activity if children need more support by making the number with place value cards and/or an abacus.)

3 Relate the work to coins, for example 10p and 4p is 14p.

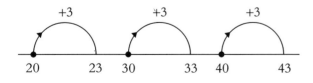

Teacher-independent activities

Choose from:

1   Start some patterns on Resource sheet 11 and ask the children to continue them.

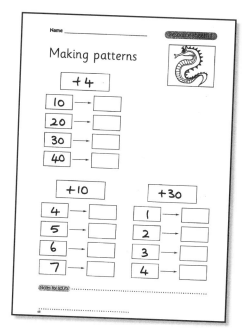

2   Use Resource sheet 12 to make a 'Three in a row' game. The children take turns to spin the spinner and choose a number from the chest to add to it in order to cover a number in the grid. The first to cover three numbers in a row in the winner.

3   Fill in the fish on Resource sheet 5 with numbers to suit the dice or spinners you use. For example, with a spinner marked 10 and 20 and a 1–6 dice, the fish need to be numbered 11 to 16 and 21 to 26. Give pairs of children a copy of the sheet and different coloured cubes. Ask them to take turns to spin the spinner and throw the dice, calculate the number and, if possible, cover the appropriate fish with one of their cubes. The winner is the child with the most cubes on the sheet.

4   For more written practice, use Resource sheet 24.

Plenary session

■   Use place value cards again to make 10's and 1's numbers.

■   Play the 'Three in a row' game in two teams using Blu-tack counters.

Add 9, add 10

Assessment focus

■   Can the children add 10 and 9 using a 100 square and number line?

Resources

■   a large 100 square and a number line

■   Resource sheets 9, 10, 12, 24 and 28

■   small number lines (Resource sheet 21)

■   cubes and spinners

With the whole class

■   Spend time adding 10 to numbers, using a 100 square to show the vertical pattern. It is crucial that all the children can add 10 to any number up to 100 for the lesson on adding 9 to make any sense.

■   Demonstrate on a 100 square how to add 10 and step back one to add 9. Repeat this many times, inviting children to the front to demonstrate the calculation on the 100 square.

■ Repeat the adding 10 and stepping back one on a large number line, again inviting children to the front to draw in the jumps.

$6 + 9$
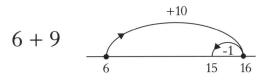

With the lower-achievers

With adult support

Choose from:

1   Repeat any of the starter activities, making sure that all the children can add 10 to any number confidently. Use 100 squares and make 0 to 99 squares (Resource sheets 9 and 10).

2   Fill in Resource sheet 28 as shown below and work with the children to complete the hops.

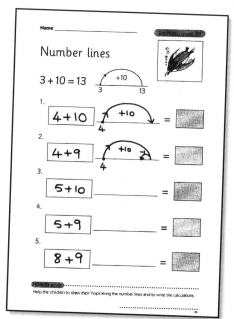

Teacher-independent activities

Choose from:

1   Let the children complete Resource sheet 28 filled in with different numbers.

2   For more written practice, let them use Resource sheet 24.

3   Use the 'Three in a row' game on Resource sheet 12 to consolidate the learning. The spinner should say 'add 10' and 'add 9'. The children should play in pairs, each with their own colour cubes, taking turns to spin the spinner. They choose a number from the treasure chest to add 10 or 9 to and then cover that number on the board with one of their cubes. The winner is the first to have a row of 3 cubes in any direction.

Plenary session

■ *"Someone tell us a quick way to add 9 that we have been learning about today."*

■ *"What did you enjoy doing today? What would you like more practice with?"*

■ Play a 'Three in a row' game in two teams, but instead of adding 10 and adding 9, just add 9 every time and observe who needs more help with that.

Add three numbers

Assessment focus

■ Can the children begin to add three numbers?

Resources

■ large number cards

■ Resource sheets 13, 27 and 29

■ dominoes, dice and three large dice

■ three 1–3 spinners

■ Blu-tack, cubes and counters

■ a timer

With the whole class

■ Talk about how you can make adding three numbers together easier if two of the numbers can be added together to make 10. Give the children an example. *"For example, to add 7 and 4 and 3, add the 7 and the 3 to make 10 first of all, then add 4 more."* Demonstrate this a few times using large number cards and then ask individuals out to the front to work on a few similar additions.

■ Play 'Three Hand Wizz'. Invite three children to the front. Explain that on the count of three, they must each show one hand with some fingers held up, and the rest of the class will try to calculate the total. Look at the three numbers with the class to see if you can make 10, or find a double, to make the addition easier. Then add the three numbers together, suggesting that the children put one of the numbers in their head and count on.

■ Throw three large dice and share strategies for how to add them (finding doubles or near doubles, and so on). Write out the calculations, for example 3 + 5 + 1 = 9. Use a large version of the three dice game on Resource sheet 29 and play in two teams. If you use three 1–6 dice, you will need the numbers 3 to 18 on the puffer fish. The teams should take it in turns to throw all three dice, add the numbers together and cover the total with their colour counter, stuck to the sheet with Blu-tack. The winning team is the one with the most numbers covered after a set time, say five or ten minutes.

■ Work with the children to complete Resource sheet 27.

With the lower-achievers

With adult support

Choose from:

1 Continue to throw three dice, using numbers to suit your children. Observe who is still counting from one each time. Talk to them about the strategies they are using.

2 Place a set of dominoes face down and go around the group asking children to take a domino and add the two numbers shown to a third number found by throwing a dice. Again, talk about the strategies.

3 Find all the doubles dominoes and give children some practice in learning their doubles to 6.

Teacher-independent activities

Choose from:

1 Give a pair of children three spinners each marked 1, 2 and 3 and let them play a race game on Resource sheet 13. They should place their counters on the head of the snake and take

turns to spin the three spinners and add together the resulting numbers. Both partners should agree that the numbers have been added correctly. Then the child can move their counter the appropriate number of spaces along the snake. The winner is the first to reach the end.

2 Fill in a copy of Resource sheet 29 as shown below for use with three spinners marked 1, 2 and 3. Give the children a sheet each, and tell them to take turns to spin all three spinners, add the numbers and cover the resulting number on the resource sheet with a cube or counter. They could also write their calculations at the bottom of the sheet. The winner is the player with the most numbers covered after 10 minutes.

Plenary session

■ *"Tell us some of the strategies you used when you added three numbers."* (Find doubles, find a pair of numbers that make 10, put the largest number in the head and count on, etc.)

■ Play 'Three Hand Wizz' again.

■ See Chapter 5 for more addition activities.

Subtraction

Overall learning objectives

- Understand subtraction as counting back, taking away and finding differences, and use the related vocabulary.
- Understand the '–' symbol and use a range of strategies for subtraction.

Key words

take away	one less
leaves	two fewer
subtract	how many fewer is ... than ...?
cross out	
how many have gone?	difference between
	is the same as

Counting back

Assessment focus

- Can the children count back on the number line and on fingers (including crossing the 10's boundary)?

Resources

- Resource sheets 6, 9, 10, 13, 21, 30, 31, 32 and 34
- a large floor number track and small individual number tracks
- 'count back' cards ('count back 2' and so on)
- counters, dice, spinners, number cards
- a 100 square
- a drum, a small plastic frog and a timer (all optional)

With the whole class

- Help the children to chant numbers from 20 back to 1. Do this in a range of ways, such as to the beat of a drum, whispering or shouting numbers, or saying them in a silly voice. Repeat

this over several days/weeks until all the children are confident.

- Using a large floor number track to at least 20, ask individuals to stand on a number and count back as they take steps. For example, *"Iqbal, stand on 16, count back 5, land on 11."* Repeat the process with fingers taking 'steps' on small number lines or tracks (such as Resource sheet 21).

- Ask the children to shut their eyes and see the number track in their head. *"Imagine you are standing on 13. Now count back 5 in your head. Where do you land?"* This crosses the 10's boundary, so make sure they know they should check all their calculations. Show them how to check by starting on 8 and adding 5 (using either fingers or steps on the number track) to make sure they get back to 13.

With the lower-achievers

With adult support

Choose from:

1 Play the 'Seashore' game using Resource sheet 30, some counters and shuffled 'count back' cards. Let the children play in pairs, starting with their counters on the 20. Explain that they should take turns turning over a card and follow the instruction. So if the first card is 'count back 3' the child should move their counter to 17. The first child to reach home wins.

2 Use Resource sheet 30 with pairs of children, counters, and a 7–12 spinner. The players take turns to spin the spinner, say what 1 less than the number shown would be and cover the relevant webbed footprint with a counter. Ask the children which footprints will not be covered if they use this spinner. Repeat the game with the children saying the number that is 2, 3 and 4 less than the number shown.

3 Using small number tracks and/or Resource sheet 31, observe all the children individually taking steps with their fingers back on a number track/line. You can generate numbers for Resource sheet 31 using dice, spinners or cards. Include some that cross the 10's boundary, such as 15 – 7. As you observe them doing these, remind them to check each time, either making their fingers take steps along the line or just counting on with fingers.

4 When the children have had plenty of experience counting back, show them how to count back 10 in one jump on a 100 square and how to use counting back 10 to count back 9 by jumping back 10 then counting on 1. This can be recorded on Resource sheet 34 and needs careful adult supervision.

Teacher-independent activities

Choose from:

1 The 'Seashore' game on Resource sheet 30 can be played by throwing a 1–6 dice and counting back. The first child to reach home wins.

2 Let the children use Resource sheet 32 with their fingers or a plastic frog to help them with counting back.

3 Use Resource sheet 13 as a race game for counting back from 50.

4 Fill in Resource sheet 6 as shown below to make a simple race game. The children can use the 'count back' cards if they are capable of reading the instructions for themselves, or use symbols on a spinner, for example '–3'. For a longer game involving racing back from 100, use Resource sheet 9.

5 Challenge the children to race to write numbers from 100 back to 1 in order on Resource sheet 10. You could set a timer and then repeat the

activity the next day to see if they can beat their personal time.

Plenary session

■ Enlarge Resource sheet 31 and do some counting back, inviting children to the front to draw in the steps.

■ *"When you go back on the number track, do the numbers get larger or smaller?"*

■ *"What have you learned today? Did you enjoy playing your maths game? Show us how you play it."*

■ *"When I counted back 5, I ended up on number 7. Where did I start?"*

Take it away

Assessment focus

■ Can the children understand subtraction as taking away and crossing out?

Resources

■ Resource sheets 35, 36 and 67
■ cubes
■ 'take away' cards and Blu-tack
■ calculators
■ a 100 square
■ a floor number line

With the whole class

■ Show the children how to find subtraction facts by folding down fingers. Say, for example, *"I am holding up 10 fingers and now I'm folding down 4, which leaves 6 standing up."* Write the calculation on the board ($10 - 4 = 6$).

■ Model subtractions with cubes. Give each child 10 cubes. Ask them to lay their cubes out in a line or in two sets of 5. Ask them questions, such as *"10 take away 5 leaves how many?"* Make sure the children have plenty of practical experience actually taking away cubes. Ask some of them to come to the front to write their calculations on the board. Then show them how to check their work.

$$10 - 6 = 4 \quad so \quad 6 + 4 = 10$$

If 10 take away 6 leaves 4, then 6 plus 4 must equal 10.

■ Give the children plenty of experience with a calculator so that they can identify the '–' and '=' keys and experiment with larger numbers. Show them how if 10 – 6 = 4, then 20 – 6 = 14, 30 – 6 = 24 and so on, finding the numbers on a 100 square.

With the lower-achievers

With adult support

Choose from:

1 Repeat the taking away with cubes, asking each child in turn to record a subtraction with 'take away' cards, sticking them with Blu-tack to a board.

2 Make the link from 'take away' to the '–' symbol using calculators. Ask the children to record subtractions on the board using the '–' symbol and doing this alongside actually taking cubes away and using the appropriate language. *"I have 12 cubes and I'm taking away 6."*

3 Show the children how to count out cubes onto the pictures on Resource sheet 35 and then take away and enter the answer. (Do some taking away with large numbers of cubes to remind them that if they had to take away a large number of cubes, such as 24, from 30 cubes, it would be quicker to take away 2 cubes at a time, counting from 2 up to 24.)

4 Some children seem to find 'crossing out' a useful way of thinking of subtraction, so draw some simple pictures on the board and let children cross out specific numbers of items, as on Resource sheet 36, making the link to the language of subtraction and to calculators.

5 Write a subtraction fact on the board and ask the children to read it. Ask *"Will the answer be more or less than the starting number?"* Establish that it will be less as we have to take something away. Demonstrate how to work out the answer using a number line. For example, for 8 – 5 = 3 you might say *"8 is the starting number, so we start on 8, jump back 5 and we end up on 3."* (Using a large floor number line here would be ideal.) Write more subtractions on the board and let the children take turns to use the number line to find the answers.

Teacher-independent activities

Choose from:

1 Let children continue to use 'take away' cards to make calculations, writing down the answers so they can bring them to the plenary session.

2 Once the children have had plenty of practical experience, they can work independently on Resource sheets 35 and 36 using cubes.

3 You can make more 'take away' worksheets by using the clip art pictures from Resource sheet 67.

Plenary session

■ Show the whole class how to do crossing out to take away. Let some children come to the front to demonstrate by drawing simple shapes such as circles then crossing through them to take some away.

■ *"What is 9 take away 4? How would you find out 9 – 4 using the large floor number line?"* (You need to make this link from subtraction to counting back repeatedly to be sure the children grasp that counting back means subtraction.)

■ *"When you do subtractions, is the number you start with more or fewer than the number you end up with?"* (Establish that you end up with a smaller number.)

Patterns in subtraction

Assessment focus

- Can the children recognise simple patterns in subtraction?

Resources

- Resource sheets 1, 2, 5, 11, 18, 21, 29, 33 and 69
- a large 100 square and number line
- cubes, dice and spinners
- a selection of equipment that is suitable for subtractions

With the whole class

- Do some counting back in 1's, 2's and 10's (and 5's when the children are ready), pointing to the numbers on a large 100 square. Write on the board the simple patterns you can get from counting back. Ask the children to predict the next number in the sequence. Ask some of them to come and write the next calculation on the board.

$17 - 10 = 7$	$9 - 1 = 8$
$27 - 10 = 17$	$10 - 1 = 9$
$37 - 10 = 27$	$11 - 1 = 10$
$47 - 10 = 37$	$12 - 1 = 11$

- Find number patterns by hopping back on a large class number line, asking the children to follow the patterns on small number lines made using Resource sheet 21. Relate these patterns to those on the large 100 square.

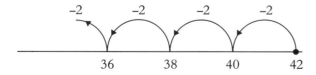

- Sit the children in a circle. Say "First we will do the addition number bonds for 8, then 18, then we are going to move on to learn the subtraction facts for 18." Play 'Ping Pong' to 8. Invite a child to come to the front and hold up a large 8 card. Ask the child (or do it yourself) to call out one number at a time, 8 or less. The other children have to reply with a number that makes it up to 8. For example, if you say "5", they must say "3" and so on. Say "We are now going to play 'Ping Pong' to 18. If 4 + 4 = 8, what would we add to 14 to make 18?" Establish the pattern by writing a few examples on the board. Then play 'Ping Pong' to 18. Explain that knowing the number partners makes doing subtractions easier.

- Put out 18 cubes and take 5 away. Write this on the board and count what is left. Tell the children that if they knew that 5 and 13 were number partners to 18, there would be no need to count. Repeat this with other examples, asking individual children to answer and write the calculations. Remind the children that a subtraction fact for 18 will always have 18 as its starting number.

With the lower-achievers

With adult support

Choose from:

1 Repeat any of the starter activities.

2 Give the children copies of Resource sheet 5. Working with any number, such as 8, ask them to take turns to pick a number card from 8 upwards (Resource sheets 1 and 2). Ask them to subtract 8 from this number, using the number line if necessary and write the answer on a fish. For example, if they take 13, they subtract 8 and write 5 on a fish. Once all the fish are filled in, let them continue taking cards but this time crossing off the answer if it is on any of their fish. The first child to cross off all the numbers is the winner.

Teacher-independent activities

Choose from:

1 Prepare copies of Resource sheet 29 as shown overleaf. Make two dice/spinners, one with larger numbers, such as 9 to 14, and the other

with smaller numbers, such as 1 to 4. Explain to the children that they play in pairs. They take turns to spin each spinner, take the smaller number number away from the larger one and then cross out the answer if it is written inside a puffer fish. There is space for them to record their calculations on the sheet. The winner is the first to cross out all their fish.

2   Use Resource sheets 11 and/or 33 to show simple patterns such as subtract 2 or subtract 10.

3   Let the children choose apparatus to work with and then ask them to record all the subtraction facts for a given number using Resource sheet 33. Write the starter numbers on the sheet yourself if necessary. Use the clip art pictures on Resource sheet 69 to make the sheet look different from the last time you used it. Alternatively, let the children do the activity with a 'train' of cubes and record it on Resource sheet 18.

Plenary session

- *"Someone tell me one of the words for subtraction."*
- *"What really made you think today?"*
- *"Come to the front, Darren, and help us to play 'Ping Pong' to 8."*
- *"Go on with my counting back pattern, 28, 26, 24, 22…"*
- *"Do you enjoy number patterns?"*
- See also Chapter 5 for more subtraction work.

Linking addition and subtraction

Overall learning objectives

- Understand that subtraction is the inverse of addition, link counting on and counting back on the number line, and use a range of language for addition and subtraction.

- Find a total when one group of objects is hidden and use symbols to stand for the unknown number.

- Halve and double numbers.

Key words

count on/back

back to where you started

how many more to make ...?

difference between

how many are left over?

how many fewer is ...?

Empty boxes

Assessment focus

- Can the children solve empty box problems (such as $3 + \square = 5$)?

Resources

- a stopwatch
- cubes and a container
- a selection of small toys, such as soft toy kittens, a basket and a cloth
- an overhead projector (optional)
- a number line, number cards and Blu-tack
- Resource sheets 18, 37 and 38

With the whole class

- Play 'Beat the Clock' to 8 (or whatever number suits your children). Sit the children in a circle or horseshoe. Tell them that they are going to try to beat the clock. Resetting the stopwatch each time, go all round the class, asking the children to answer as quickly as they can with the 'partner' of 8 for whatever number you say. (So if you say *"3"*, the child must reply *"5".*) If some of the lower-achievers seem worried about this game, let them reply in pairs or small groups. Play again, encouraging them to try to beat their previous time. Then repeat the game with 18, making links between 3 + 5 and 13 + 5 and so on.

- Play the 'Missing Cubes' game. Place 8 cubes on the overhead projector or in the middle of the circle and ask a child to count them. Tell the children to close their eyes. Then take away some of the cubes and hide them in a container. Say *"Open your eyes. Mary, count how many are left. So how many did I take away? How did you work that out? Did anyone work it out in a different way? Let's do it again and this time try to think very carefully about what you did in your head to work it out."* Repeat the process, this time concealing a different number of cubes in the container. The children will have a range of ways to work out the difference. Write the relevant calculations on the board and ask individual children to read them out.

  $8 - \square$ (read this as 'something') makes 5.

  $5 + \square$ equals 8.

  It is crucial that the children see a range of ways of writing equations. Repeat this for 18 cubes.

- Play 'Kittens in a Basket' (or 'Fish in a Treasure Chest', 'Cookies in a Jar' or 'Cubes in a Bag'). Show the children 8 small toys (or whatever number you are working with) to represent the kittens. Hide the kittens in a basket concealed with a cloth, so that the children cannot see into it. Take out two of the kittens. Say *"Two kittens have come out to play. How many are hiding in the basket? How did you work that out?"*

With the lower-achievers

With adult support

Choose from:

1   Using a class number line, highlight the number you are working with. Write up an empty box sum on the board for that number bond, such as $5 + \square = 8$. Explain that the missing number is the difference between the two numbers and tell them that you are going to jump along the

number line to find out what it is. Show them how to jump on, reminding them to stop at the finishing number. *"6, 7, 8. That is 3 jumps. Therefore the missing number is 3."* Repeat the process with different numbers and let the children take turns. They can record this by sticking number cards with Blu-tack onto a board and share it later in the plenary session.

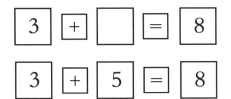

2   Adapt the 'Kittens in a Basket' game to provide some other context, such as using Play People. Let the children take turns hiding the astronauts in the spaceship, bees in the hive and so on.

3   Work with the children to complete Resource sheet 38. Point out that we can use any symbol we want to stand for our missing or secret number. Read the sentences as *"5 and something makes 6. What is the something?"* Show how it can be worked out using a number line and encourage the children to 'see' the number line in their head.

Teacher-independent activities

Choose from:

1   Make sure you give the children plenty of experience with number bonds to 10. Let them work in pairs to play the 'Missing Cubes' game again, but this time with 10 cubes, letting them take turns to put cubes in the pot.

2   Prepare copies of Resource sheet 37. This can be done with any number of fish from 8 upwards.

3   The activity can be repeated in a slightly different way by splitting up a cube 'train' of any number and recording the results on Resource sheet 18.

Plenary session

■   *"4 add what makes 8?"*

■   *"What would I add to 6 to make 8?"*

■   *"Who knows some of the number bonds of 8, 10, 15, 18, 20 by heart?"*

■   Play 'Ping Pong' with a number you have worked with that day. For example, if it is 'Ping Pong' to 10, ask a child to stand at the front holding a large 10 number card. You or the child should say a number and the class should respond with the partner number to 10. If you say *"6"* they must reply *"4"*.

Count on, count back

Assessment focus

■   Can the children link counting on to addition and counting back to subtraction (and find the difference between two numbers)?

Resources

■   floor or wall number lines and 100 squares

■   cubes, counters, spinners

■   Resource sheets 5, 7, 12, 13, 19, 28, 29, 39, 40 and 69

■   'count back' cards, such as 'count back 2'

■   subtraction cards

With the whole class

You will want to do the different aspects of this lesson on different days.

■   Demonstrate how to count on and count back on a large floor or wall number line. Make sure the children understand that to count on we move to the right as the numbers get bigger, and to count back we move to the left and the numbers get smaller. Relate counting on and counting back to addition and subtraction, doing some actual combining of two or more sets to model addition and doing some physical taking away to clarify subtraction. Relate what you are doing to a 100 square. (Note that a 100 square is often not as good as a number line for children to use when calculating on their own, as they tend to make errors going from the end of one line of the square to the start of the next one. Adding 10 or 9 or 11, the 100 square is ideal.)

- *"So what is 3 count on 7? Come and show us how you can do that on a number line."*

- On the large floor number line, show how if you start on 7 and take a step of 3 you land on 10, and if you then count back 3 you end up back on 7. Make as much of the 'magic' of this as you can as it is a fundamental concept in linking addition and subtraction. Repeat many examples over several days. Keep coming back to this over the next few weeks in mental maths time. Show how the hop forward and back can be recorded as on Resource sheet 40.

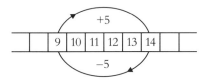

- Demonstrate also how to find a small difference by counting up from the lower number to the higher.

- Use cube 'trains' to show how you can find differences by matching the 'trains' and looking at the bit left over at the end (which you can break off).

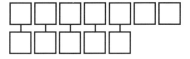

"So the difference between 7 and 5 is 2. Your brother is 5. You are 7. The difference in your ages is 2 years."

With the lower-achievers

With adult support

Choose from:

1   Repeat any of the starter activities. You will need to give the children plenty of experience with finding differences. You will probably need to work with them to do Resource sheet 39.

2   Find small differences by counting up on a large number line then record this using Resource sheet 28 with calculations to suit your children.

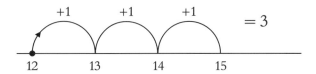

3   Using the 'Bingo/Lotto' cards on Resource sheet 7, ask the children to fill in numbers 1 to 10. Call out calculations with answers between 1 and 10, for example *"What is the difference between 3 and 5?"* In this instance, the children with a 2 on their card can cover it with a counter. The first child to cover a row (or the whole card) wins.

Teacher-independent activities

Choose from:

1   Fill in Resource sheets 5 or 19 with numbers 1 to 10 or to suit your children. Explain that they must join any fish (or seal) with a difference of 2 (or to suit your children). So, the fish with number 1 in it will be joined to the fish with number 3 in it and so on.

2   Complete Resource sheet 40 as shown below. You will probably have to work with the children initially to do the counting on and back on it, but then you can use a different picture from the clip art from Resource sheet 69 and fill in different numbers and let them use the sheet again, working independently.

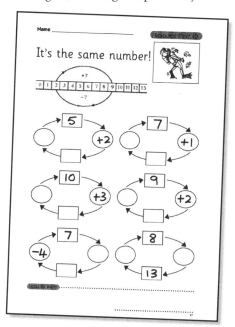

3   Use Resource sheet 12 to make a 'Three in a Row' game. Write some numbers in the treasure chest and some on the spinner. The children should take turns to spin the spinner and choose a number from the treasure chest. They then cover the difference between the

two numbers with their colour cube. The first child to have a line of three of their cubes in any direction is the winner.

4   Using Resource sheet 13 and 'count back' or subtraction cards, let the children take turns to turn over a card and move counters back along the snake, starting from 50. The first child to reach the snake's tail is the winner.

Plenary session

■   *"Tell me one way that you can find the difference between two numbers. Is there another way to work out differences?"*

■   *"Who can tell me a maths word that is to do with taking away?"*

■   Make a 'taking away' poster with the children. Add to it any new words as you go along.

Taking Away

difference between
counting back
subtraction
minus
counting out

Enlarge Resource sheet 29. Fill in the puffer fish with numbers that will be generated by the difference between the spinners you want to use. So, with two 1–10 spinners, your differences will be between 10 and 1, so your highest number will be 9 and your lowest will be 0. Divide the class into two teams, each with their own colour counters. Let them take turns to spin both spinners, work out the difference and then cover that number with their colour counter. The winning team is the one with the most counters on the board at the end.

Double and halve

Assessment focus

■   Can the children double and halve numbers up to 20 (and use that in calculating)?

Resources

■   Resource sheets 1, 2, 24, 29, 41, 42, 43, 44 and 69

■   dominoes, cubes, counters, dice, spinners

■   a 1–10 spinner

With the whole class

You will want to teach the different aspects of this lesson on different days. Note that there are links to doubling covered in Chapter 6.

■   Show some dominoes and ask the children what 'doubles' are. Go over doubles to 10 (or 20) with plenty of repetition so that lower-achievers have time to learn the numbers. Link doubling to multiplying by 2 by showing '2 lots of' cubes.

Doubling is finding 2 lots of the same number. So, double 6 is 2 lots of 6 which is 12.

■   Show how 2 lots of 6 cubes can be split again so that you find half of 12. Give plenty of practical experience with small groups finding halves of cube 'trains'. Make a list on the board of what they find. (You will need to come back to doubling and halving when you do the 2 times table.)

double 1 is 2   half of 2 is 1
double 2 is 4   half of 4 is 2
3 + 3 = 6   half of 6 is 3
4 + 4 = 8

■ Enlarge Resource sheet 41 and fill it in as shown below. Put a counter on the first space (6). Target individuals with questions about what you need to do to 6 to get to the next space, which is 12. (They could say add 6, or double 6 or times 2.) Then ask another child or group of children how to get from 12 to 10. (Take away 2.) Go around the board like this, telling the children you want them to focus particularly on doubles and halves. Play the game again but in reverse, starting at the 9 and moving to 18. Talk about how the game is different when played in this direction. *"What do you do to the numbers if you go round this way?"*

■ Once some doubles have been learned, give experience of adding doubles and near doubles, for example 6 + 6 and 6 + 7. Ask the children to explain how they did their calculations, remembering to try to elicit a whole range of ways to calculate. Show them also how to use halving or 'near halving', for example 10 – 5 or 14 – 6, and using larger numbers that they are familiar with, such as 100 – 50 and 100 – 49.

With the lower-achievers

With adult support

Choose from:

1 Using dominoes, ask the children to sort out which are the doubles. (You need to be sure that everyone understands the word!) Ask them

to work in pairs and count the dots and draw the domino doubles (or record them on Resource sheet 42).

2 Give more practical experience with cube 'trains' finding halves and doubles. Allow more time to help the children learn their doubles to 10 (or 20) by heart.

3 Use Resource sheet 43. The first time you use it, you will probably need to work with the children, but you can use it again with a different clip art picture from Resource sheet 69 and larger numbers.

4 To make sure children understand what 'near doubles' are, ask them to put out number cards (from Resource sheets 1 and 2) in pairs that are 'near each other', for example the 6 and the 5 together. Give experience with using near doubles for calculating, for example adding 4 and 5 by doubling 4 and adding 1. You could use Resource sheet 24 to record these.

Teacher-independent activities

Choose from:

1 Let the children work with Resource sheets 42 and 43 using larger numbers.

2 Let the children share or have individual copies of Resource sheet 44 filled in as shown below. (You might find you need to enlarge the seal for some children and just let them use one picture at a time.) They spin the spinner (see

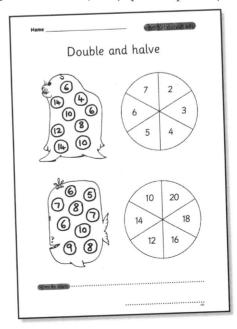

page 4), double the number and then cover that number on their animal with a counter. The first child to cover all their numbers is the winner. The second game is played in the same way, but this time the children have to halve the number on the spinner. Both games can be played with other numbers using different dice or spinners.

3   For more practice, fill in the puffer fish on Resource sheet 29 with even numbers, for example 2 to 20, with some repeats. Give the children a 1–10 spinner, and let them take turns to spin it, double their number and cover the appropriate fish with a counter. Alternatively, you could ask the children to write their calculations in the space at the bottom of the sheet and write in the doubled number they make on a fish. They should continue to play until all the fish are filled in, then go on playing, but this time crossing out their doubled numbers. The first to cross out all of their numbers is the winner.

Plenary session

■   *"What did you enjoy today?"*

■   *"Who knows all their doubles to 10 by heart?"*

■   *"What would you like more practice with?"*

■   *"What is your favourite maths game? Could you think of some different rules that we could use for that game?"*

■   *"Why does doubling help us to calculate quickly? What is the opposite of doubling?"*

Maths around the world

Assessment focus

■   Can the children use a range of addition and subtraction strategies (and recall rapidly addition and subtraction facts)?

Resources

■   cubes, counters and dice

■   place value cards

■   coins

■   Resource sheets 16, 41, 45, 46, 47, 48 and 49

■   a pack of playing cards

With the whole class

■   Partitioning into 5 and a bit can be difficult for lower-achievers. Give plenty of experience with finger patterns up to 10. They can learn numbers 5 to 10 as '5 and a bit', for example 6 is 5 + 1 and 7 is 5 + 2. Show both hands with fingers up, but always with one hand showing all 5 fingers. Establish that one hand is 5 so they just have to count the other fingers. Stress that just in the way that they learned to 'see' the domino patterns of numbers (Resource sheets 3 and 4) and learn them by heart, so they can learn their '5 and a bit' numbers by heart.

■   Demonstrate how to split the numbers 6 to 9 for adding with '5 and a bit'.

$$5 + 6$$
$$5 + 5 + 1$$
$$10 + 1 = 11$$

$$7 + 9$$
$$5 + 2 + 5 + 4$$
$$10 + 6 = 16$$

■   The other important partitioning of numbers is into tens and units. Recap on this with place value cards. Show the children how to split 2 two-digit numbers into tens and units and then recombine them, using place value cards from Resource sheet 16 and 10p and 1p coins.

■ When the children have experienced a range of mental methods with addition and subtraction, give them a selection of calculations and ask them to put them in groups.

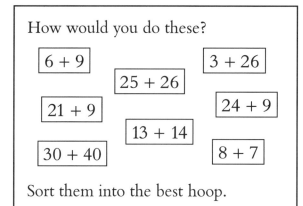

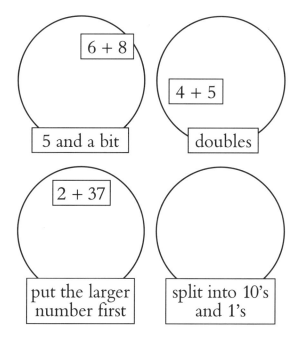

You might want just to work with two different strategies at first.

■ Play 'Maths Around the World'. Ask the children to stand behind their chairs in a circle. One child goes inside the circle and faces another child. Ask the pair an addition or subtraction fact, such as *"What is 3 + 5?"* (Ask questions that you know your lower-achievers can answer, such as *"Show me a '5 and a bit' number with two hands,"* or let some children answer as a pair.) The first of the two children facing each other to call out the correct answer

wins and the other sits down. If they both answer correctly at the same time, play again until one wins. The winner moves on to the next child in the circle. This continues until every child has had a go and the last child standing is the winner.

With the lower-achievers

With adult support

Choose from:

1 Say *"I'm going to say one of your names and give you a number and you must say its partner."* For example, if you are working on 8 you might say *"John, 7."* John has to say the number bond partner (1). If the child is stuck, remind them how to count on to find the partner. Continue until they have had a few goes each.

2 Play 'Maths Around the World' using addition and subtraction facts for just one number, then gradually extend this to a whole range of numbers and different strategies.

3 Play 'Number Bond Snap' using a pack of playing cards. Use four picture cards to represent 0 and remove all the other picture cards and all the cards above the bond you are working on. So, if you are working with number bonds of 8 take out all the 9's and 10's. Share the cards evenly between the children, and let them take turns to put one card onto a central pile. If the last two numbers add up to 8 (or the number bond you are working on), the first child to shout *"8!"* wins the pile of cards. Each time there is winner, ask the children for a number fact for the two cards and write it on the board. The winner wins all the cards.

4 Use Resource sheet 46 with the children to record tens and units additions.

5 Show the children how to complete addition squares, using Resource sheet 47.

Teacher-independent activities

Choose from:

1 Give children copies of Resource sheet 45 to work on the '5 and a bit' numbers. The sheet includes space for them to do some simple '5 and a bit' adding, and also for some children to move onto 15 + 6, and so on.

2   Fill in some numbers from 0 up to the number bond you are practising on Resource sheet 41, for example 0 to 10 for bonds to 10. Ask the children to take turns to throw a dice and move counters on the appropriate number of spaces. Whatever number they land on, they must say the number they would need to add to it to make 10. For example, if they land on 6, they must say 4. If all the players agree that the child has said the right number, the child wins that number of cubes. The winner is the player with the most cubes when they have all reached the end of the track. If a child needs extra practice in counting, they could count the cubes at the plenary session and announce the winner.

3   Resource sheet 48 is a consolidation activity to do in pairs. Choose a target number and put it in the middle of the circle. Challenge the children to work together to split the number into two on the top target and into three on the bottom one in as many ways as they can. Point out that they can use 0 or repeated numbers as necessary.

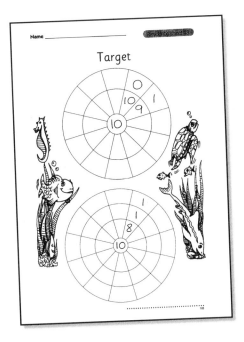

4   Resource sheet 49 filled in as shown above right is another consolidation activity that can be used to develop children's ability to add three numbers. (See also Chapter 3.) Let them play in pairs with their own colour cubes. They take turns to find a group of three numbers that form a line or group to make 20, for example 1

+ 2 + 17. They cover those three numbers with their cubes. Make more games like this, including the addition of just two numbers to make 10 if they need that support.

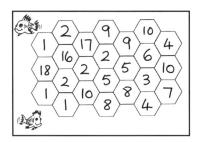

Plenary session

- *"Shout out the number of fingers I'm holding up."*
- *"Someone explain how to add 7 and 9 using the '5 and a bit' method."*
- *"What do you think would be the best adding strategy to use to add 12 and 13?"*
- *"Shut your eyes and try to 'see' your number line you keep in your head. Stand on number 6. How many do you need to jump to get to 12?"*
- *"Tell me three numbers that add up to 20."*

Magic numbers

Assessment focus

- Can the children make an addition and subtraction fact from three given numbers in the 0 to 20 range?

Resources

- Resource sheets 1, 2, 50 and 51
- number lines and cubes
- a black pen and Blu-tack

With the whole class

- Some lower-achievers find it hard to make links between pieces of their knowledge, and they can find it hard to use what they know to find new number facts. Display large number cards 4, 3 and 7 (from Resource sheet 1), and write on the board $4 + 3 = 7$. Ask the children to make a 'train' of 7 cubes. Ask *"What can we also work out if we know 4 + 3 = 7?"* (Some children are likely to say $2 + 5 = 7$, so explain that today we are not splitting up 7, but thinking about our 'magic three numbers' 3, 4 and 7.) Show how you can make two additions and two subtractions with those same three numbers.

$$4 + 3 = 7 \qquad 7 - 4 = 3$$
$$3 + 4 = 7 \qquad 7 - 3 = 4$$

■ Give plenty of time to helping the children make those links between addition and subtraction and develop an understanding of the range of language they need to be able to use. Cut out the words from an enlarged copy of Resource sheet 50 to develop the 'magic three numbers' activity by making sentences using a range of language, such as 'The difference between 7 and 3 is 4.' As the children gain in confidence, use a bold black pen to make more word cards using the spaces provided, for example to make the sentences '7 is 4 more than 3' and '3 is 4 fewer than 7.' Stick up the sentences you make with Blu-tack, working with the same three numbers to begin with.

With the lower-achievers

With adult support

Choose from:

1   Repeat the whole-class activities.

2   Ask the children to think of another set of 'magic three numbers'. (If they say, for example, 4, 5 and 13, you know they have not understood!) Explain how the two lower numbers add up to make the third number.

Teacher-independent activities

Choose from:

1   Give the children the words from Resource sheet 50 and a batch of number cards for their three numbers (Resource sheets 1 and 2). Then invite them to use Blu-tack to make sentences to stick to a board.

2   Choose three numbers for the children to work with and ask them to use them to complete Resource sheet 51.

Plenary session

■ *"Read your number sentences to us."*

■ *"I'm thinking of a number and it is 5 less than 8."*

■ *"What did you learn today that was 'new knowledge' for you?"*

■ *"Who can tell me a number fact that they know by heart without having to think about it? If you learn lots of those number facts you will get much better at maths."*

■ *"Could I do 'magic three numbers' with 4, 5 and 7?"* (No)

■ *"If 5 and 6 were my first two magic numbers, what would my third one be?"* (11)

■ *"Give me three numbers that could work to do 'magic three numbers'."*

Multiplication and division

Overall learning objectives

- Understand the operation of multiplication as repeated addition or as describing an array (and begin to see the relationship between multiplication and division).

- Know by heart multiplication facts for the 2 and 10 times tables (later 5).

Key words

lots of	repeated addition
rows of	multiply by
columns of	times
sets of	two times
groups of	ten times
double	group in pairs/tens
halve	equal groups of
array	divided by

Counting in 2's and 10's

Assessment focus

- Can the children count in 2's and 10's (later 5's)?

Resources

- a large 100 square and number line
- Resource sheets 5 and 9
- calculators
- spinners

With the whole class

- Count in 2's on the number line, chanting the numbers. Establish that each jump is a jump of 2. Repeat the process on the large 100 square.

- Ask the children to recite the 2 times table up to ten 2's, holding up their fingers, each finger representing 2.

- Go around the circle counting the children's legs in 2's.

- Show the children how to use the calculator constant by keying in 2+ = = = = so that it counts in 2's. Ask *"Will 19 show on the screen? Why not?"*

- Make the link to even numbers.

- Make the link to division by asking questions such as *"How many hops of 2 do I make to get to 10?"*

- Repeat these activities for times 10 and times 5.

With the lower-achievers

With adult support

Choose from:

1   Help the children to take jumps along the number line, again chanting the pattern of the 2's. *"Are we going to land on 20? What about 13? If I stand on 6 and take two jumps of 2, where will I land?"*

2   Go over doubles of all numbers to 10, then to 20. Clarify that double 6 is two lots of 6.

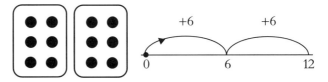

Two lots of 6 is double 6.

3   When you work on the 5 times table, show the children how the answers are half the answers in the 10 times table.

Teacher-independent activities

Choose from:

1   Using a 100 square, Resource sheet 9 and a calculator, ask the children to circle all the numbers in the 2 times table up to 100 and try to learn them to say at the plenary session.

2   Ask the children to work in pairs with just one calculator between them. They should take turns to make the calculator count in 2's and to say the numbers without looking at the calculator screen. Challenge them over about two weeks to

be able to count in 2's to 100 or above. (Make the link to even numbers and number sequences. See Chapter 1.)

3   Use Resource sheet 5 and a spinner (see page 4) with numbers to suit your children. Ask them to spin the spinner, multiply the number by 2 and write the answer on a fish. When all the fish have a number on them, they should keep playing and cross out each number. The first child to cross out all their fish wins.

Plenary session

■   *"Let's all count in 2's and go as far as we can. Can you go backwards in 2's from 18 and stop at 4?"*

■   *"Who could count in 2's with a friend?"*

■   *"Sam, come and draw five hops of 2 along this number line."*

Lots of

Assessment focus

■   Can the children make and talk about 'lots of'?

Resources

■   cubes and counters

■   Resource sheets 12 and 52

With the whole class

■   Give each child 12 cubes and ask them to set out 'three lots of 4', 'six lots of 2' and so on. Draw pictures on the board. Demonstrate how to write 'four lots of 2' so that they can use Resource sheet 52.

■   Make the links to division by saying, for example, *"Share out your 12 cubes equally into 2 groups."*

With the lower-achievers

With adult support

Choose from:

1   Give the children plenty of experience in making cubes into equal groups. *"Can I make 12 cubes into equal groups of 2? Will 14 cubes go into*

equal groups of 3?" Ask the children to each make different 'lots of' and ask them to talk about what they have done. *"I've made four lots of 2 and that is 8 altogether: 2, 4, 6, 8. What will four lots of 5 look like? Make it with your cubes."*

2   Lay out the 2 times table in cubes, using one lot of 2, two lots of 2 and so on. Help the children to count them and again recite the numbers.

3   Use Resource sheet 52 for the children to record on. Choose a number of cubes to work with, for example 8, 9, 10, 12, 15, 18 or 24, and let the children stick to that one number for the whole of their sheet. (So if you choose 15, they can make three lots of 5, five lots of 3, 15 lots of 1 and one lot of 15.) Make sure that the children understand that five lots of 3 is 3 five times and not 5 plus 3.

Teacher-independent activities

Choose from:

1   Let the children make 'lots of' with a pile of cubes and record these in pictures in their own way or on Resource sheet 52. This time they can have a different number of cubes for each picture or you can choose for them. Stress that each time they must make equal groups.

2   Ask the children to play 'Three in a Row' on Resource sheet 12. Let them play in pairs or two teams using two colours of counters. They take turns to choose a number from the chest or from the circle, multiply it by 2 and then cover that number on the grid. The first to make three in a row in any direction wins.

Later, you can adapt Resource sheet 12 for division by putting the multiples of 2 in the treasure chest and on the spinner, then 2, 4, 6, 8 and so on on the grid. Demonstrate with cubes how three lots of 4 can be 12 shared into equal groups of 3 or 4, or into 12 lots of 1.

Plenary session

■ Draw some pictures of 'lots of' on the board. Say *"Someone come and tell me about my pictures."*

■ *"Who would like to come and draw some 'lots of' on the board?"*

■ *"Shut your eyes and try to make a picture of three lots of 2 in your head. How many cubes do you need? Make sure all your groups are equal."*

Arrays

Assessment focus

■ Can the children describe and make arrays and begin to see that multiplication can be done in any order?

Resources

■ Resource sheet 53

■ cubes

■ pegboards

■ squared paper

■ number cards and task cards for making arrays

■ workbooks, scissors, glue

With the whole class

■ Use 12 cubes to demonstrate making three lots of 4 as an array as shown on Resource sheet 53. Draw the array on the board and ask the children to talk about the rows and columns. Then change the array to four lots of 3. Draw several more arrays on the board. Let the children make their own arrays with cubes or by drawing them. It is important to model the way the children will be working when they work on Resource sheet 53.

■ Give plenty of practical experience with making arrays with cubes. *"Make an array of two lots of 5. Make 5 rows of 2."* Each time show how you can multiply in any order, for example 2 x 5 gives the same answer as 5 x 2.

■ Put out 10 cubes and ask how many there are. Tell the class that you are going to put the cubes in groups of 2. Then ask someone to come to the front to put the same 10 cubes into 2 groups. Show how 5 x 2 and 2 x 5 have the same answer. Repeat for other numbers. Make the link to addition. *"Addition can be done in any order and so can multiplication."*

With the lower-achievers

With adult support

Choose from:

1   Work with the children to make arrays with cubes. *"Tell us about your array. How many rows (across)? How many columns (down)? Now change your array so that it is the other way around."*

2   Give a range of further practical experience with squared paper or pegboards, making arrays and naming them. Use a wide range of language. The children can stick arrays on squared paper into their books. You could do this with random arrays, or make the arrays for the 2, 10 or 5 times tables.

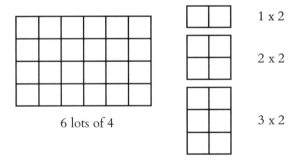

6 lots of 4

1 x 2

2 x 2

3 x 2

Use a wide range of language to describe arrays. *"2 sets of 3, 3 rows of 2, 2 columns of 3, 3 groups of 2,"* and so on.

3   Put out an even number of cubes up to 20, such as 12. Ask a child to put them in groups of 2 and tell the rest how to say this as a multiplication. *"Six lots of 2."* Then ask the child to divide them into 2 groups and ask how to write that as a multiplication. *"Two lots of 6."*

Teacher-independent activities

Choose from:

1 Let the children use Resource sheet 53. Explain that they must select their number of cubes and make their arrays, drawing them and filling in the 'lots of'. Give them cubes to work with, such as 16 to make 2 lots of 8. You might want to write the number of cubes to use or give the children number cards to choose from, for example 15, 18, 21 or 24.

2 Give the children task cards, such as '6 lots of 2' and ask them to make the arrays on pegboards or on squared paper and talk about them later at the plenary session.

Plenary session

- ◼ *"Tell me what an array looks like."*

- ◼ *"Jake, show us one of your arrays, maybe three lots of 3. What would it be the other way around? Square numbers are the same both ways round."*

- ◼ Make sure the children can use a wide range of language to talk about arrays.

- ◼ *"What is very special about the way round you do multiplication? So do you get the same answer whichever way around it is? Is addition like that?"* (Yes) *"What about subtraction?"* (No)

Enormous sums

Assessment focus

- ◼ Can the children see the relationship between repeated addition and multiplication?

Resources

- ◼ cubes and dice
- ◼ Resource sheets 54 and 55
- ◼ task cards

With the whole class

- ◼ *"Today we are going to learn more about 'lots of' and see how we could write some 'enormous sums'."* Put out three groups of 2 cubes. *"We could write this as an*

adding sum: 2 + 2 + 2 = 6." Add one more group of 2, saying, *"Four groups of 2,"* Write this as a long addition. Then five lots of 2 and so on. Say *"This type of sum is called a repeated addition, but there is a quicker way of writing it down."* Introduce the multiplication sign, 5 x 2 = 10. Repeat with other examples, asking individual children to write the repeated additions and related multiplication on the board.

- ◼ Write up some 'enormous sums' and ask the children to come and write them in a quick way using the multiplication sign. Link the related calculations with a line, as shown in the example on Resource sheet 54.

With the lower-achievers

With adult support

Choose from:

1 Tell the children that you are going to throw two dice and make up a multiplication from the resulting numbers. For example, if you throw a 6 and a 4, you will say *"6 x 4"*. Write the multiplication and show the children how to represent it with cubes and as a repeated addition 'enormous sum'. *"Tell me how to write it in a quicker way using multiplication."* Repeat the process, letting the children throw the dice and explain the sums. Record each calculation to come back to at the plenary session. *"How would we write 2 + 2 + 2 as a multiplication? How would we write 4 x 5 as a repeated addition?"*

2 Use Resource sheet 55. Count the children's fingers and write the repeated additions on the board. With two children this is 10 + 10 or 2 x 10 = 20. Go on adding 10 each time, again emphasising the 'enormous sums' and how they can be written more quickly.

3 Write 'enormous sums' linked to the 2 times table, and again, use a range of language to talk about these.

Teacher-independent activities

Choose from:

1 Let the children work in pairs to put out cubes as directed by task cards and write 'enormous sums', for example '9 lots of 2'.

2 Give children copies of Resource sheet 54 and ask them to join the related calculations.

3 Let pairs of children have 20 cubes and take it in turns to put them in equal groups of numbers and record them as repeated addition and multiplication.

4 Set the children a challenge to write the longest 'enormous sum'.

Plenary session

■ *"Read this 'enormous sum' to me," (*for example 10 add 10 add 10 add 10, and so on).

■ *"Who wrote the most 'enormous sum'?"*

■ *"What is a quick way to write multiple additions?"*

■ *"What did you learn today?"*

Two times table

Assessment focus

■ Do the children know the multiplication facts for the 2 times table?

Resources

■ a large number line to 20

■ cubes and spinners

■ Resource sheets 7, 56 and 57

With the whole class

■ Say *"Today you will be working on the 2 times table."* Begin by counting forwards in 2's up to 20 using a class number line and a row of 10 children, counting their legs or arms. Say *"This is counting in multiples of 2."* Count forwards and backwards. Stop at certain numbers and ask what is 2 more or 2 less. Say *"I'm going to write the multiples of 2 up to 20 on the board."* Write them in a downward column on the right-hand side of the board. Ask the children to chant the 2 times table to you and point to each multiple as they say it. *"1 times 2 equals 2,"* and so on.

■ Say *"If you know how to count in 2's you can work out any 2 times calculation."* Demonstrate this

using the number line and counting with fingers to find the answers. For example, *"To find 8 times 2, hold up 8 fingers and count 2, 4, 6, 8, 10, 12, 14, 16."*

■ Ask individual children to tell you how many times 2 one of the multiples on the board is, for example 12. Ask them to work it out by counting down and write the calculation. Repeat this with other numbers until the whole table is complete. Encourage the children to use clear mathematical language when writing the calculations.

■ Repeat the table a few times and suggest that they learn it at home by heart.

■ Link multiplying by 2 to doubling (see Chapter 5).

With the lower-achievers

With adult support

Choose from:

1 Recap on counting in 2's using a class number line. Give the children copies of Resource sheet 56. Make sure they understand about counting the legs on the seagulls and can link this to counting in 2's. Count something else in 2's, such as their feet or eyes.

2 Make cards from Resource sheet 57 and hold them up one at a time, making sure that the children have a strategy for working out the calculations. Check that they can talk about the card using the language of multiplication, for example *"6 lots of 2, 6 times 2, 6 multiplied by 2".* Then go through the cards again. The first child to call out the answer each time wins the card. Finish with chanting the 2 times table up to 20.

3 Using the 'Bingo' cards from Resource sheet 7, ask the children to fill in the spaces with the multiples of 2. (They will need to use some repeats.) Shuffle the cards from Resource sheet 57, and give the children cubes to cover their 'Bingo' card spaces. Turn the cards over one at a time. Call out the multiplication and ask any children with the answer on their cards to cover it with a cube. Note who can work it out and find the answer. The first child to cover a whole line in any direction wins.

Teacher-independent activities

Choose from:

1 Photocopy Resource sheet 57 onto card, cut it up and write the answers on the back of each card. (4 is on the back of 2 x 2, and so on.) Ask the children to put them answer-side up on the table and take turns to choose one and say what the calculation must be. For example, if the number is 6, the calculation must be 3 x 2. If the child is right, they win that card. Then let them repeat the game with the cards calculation-side up, saying the answer.

2 Let children work in pairs to play the '2 times game' on Resource sheet 56. Explain that they should take turns to use the spinner and find the 2 times table fact for whichever number they get, counting the legs on the seagulls in 2's and filling in the answer. The first child to have all the facts written on their sheet is the winner. Then they can test each other on the facts. The star on the spinner can be used for any number.

Plenary session

- *"Who now knows their 2 times table by heart?"*
- *"What is 3 x 2?"*
- *"Tom, come and draw two lots of 4 on the board."*
- *"Is 19 a multiple of 2?"*
- *"How many legs would 10 seagulls have?"*

10 times table

Assessment focus

- Do the children know the multiplication facts for the 10 (later 5) times table?

Resources

- Resource sheets 5, 7, 8, 11, 55 and 58
- a large 100 square and number line
- cubes and counters
- calculators
- dice or spinners

With the whole class

- Repeat the activities suggested on page 48 for the 2 times table but this time for the 10 times table. Include finding the multiples of 10 on a large 100 square as well.

- Later do the activities again for the 5 times table, but link this to halving the answers in the 10 times table.

- Play a whole-class 'Bingo' game using Resource sheet 7. Each child should fill in multiples of 10 at random, with some repeats. Call out multiplications, such as 6 x 10, and ask the children to cover the answers with a cube. The first child to cover a line in any direction wins.

With the lower-achievers

With adult support

Choose from:

1 Link multiplication to multiple addition and jumping on along the number line to be sure that is understood.

2 Ask the children to write the multiples of 10 on the fish on Resource sheet 5. Observe who understands that instruction. Then let them use a 1–10 spinner or dice to play a teacher-independent game (see activity 1 on page 50).

3 Help the children to work with Resource sheet 55, making the multiplications with cubes or counting their fingers. Find the numbers on the

number line and on the 100 square. Make the links to multiple addition, reminding the children of 'enormous sums'.

Teacher-independent activities

Choose from:

1   Let the children play a game on Resource sheet 5, by spinning a number with a 1–10 spinner, multiplying it by 10 and writing that number in a fish. When the fish all have numbers they continue to play but this time covering the fish with a counter or cube.

2   Let the children use calculators to make the multiples of 10 appear by pressing 10 + + = = = (or whatever your calculators need to count 10, 20, 30 and so on). Let them work in pairs to count as far as they can and record the number they reach.

3   Photocopy Resource sheet 58 onto card and write the answers on the back; so 2 x 10 will have 20 on the back. Put the cards answer-side up and ask the children to challenge each other to find a particular card, such as *"Find 6 times 10."* They keep any card they get right.

4   Let the children play the '10 times game' on Resource sheet 55. Tell them to spin a number on the 0–10 spinner, multiply it by 10 and fill in the answer on the times table, racing to see who can finish the sheet first.

5   Resource sheets 8 and 11 can be used for consolidation.

Plenary session

- *"Who can say their ten times table by heart?"*

- *"Let's count these 10p's in 10's. How many 10p's make £1?"*

Division on the number line

Assessment focus

- Can the children begin to see division as repeated subtraction on the number line?

Resources

- large number lines

- a Unifix number line

- Resource sheets 21, 40 and 59

- cubes

With the whole class

- Give grouping problems based on number line hops. *"If a teacher has 18 crayons, to how many children can she give 2?"* Make the link to hops along the number line. Explain how there might have been more than 9 children in the class, but only 9 of them could have 2 crayons each. The rest can't have any. Make it clear that this way of counting back along a number line to solve a division problem is different from sharing equally so that everyone has an equal share of something.

- Remind the children of repeated addition (see earlier in this chapter) and show them how it is the reverse or opposite of doing division by

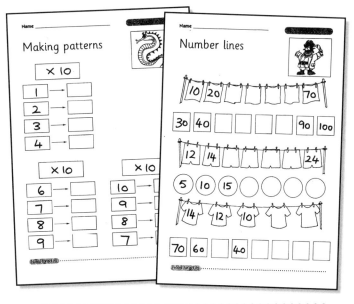

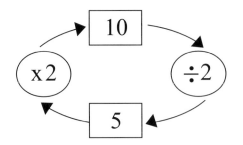

repeated subtraction. You can link multiplication to division by using Resource sheet 40.

■ Using large number lines, ask some children to the front to show how to take hops back, for example *"Start on 12 and hop back in 3's. How many hops to get to 0?"* Again, write the repeated subtraction on the board and use a wide range of language, such as *"You need 4 hops of 3 to get to 0 from 12. That is 12 subtract 3, subtract another 3, take away another 3 and another 3. That is 4 lots of 3 altogether. We learned what 3 lots of 4 was when we were doing multiplication,"* and so on.

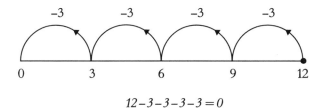

$$12 - 3 - 3 - 3 - 3 = 0$$

■ You might find it best to give equal sharing problems on a different day from division by repeated subtraction (grouping). Give practical work with cubes. For example, share out 10 cubes equally between 5 groups. Make sure all the children can at least share out using the 'one for this group, one for that group' method.

With the lower-achievers

With adult support

Choose from:

1 On a Unifix number line or similar, show how you can count back by taking away cubes in equal groups. This can be made clear by using different colours for groups of 2 (or whatever number you are using), snapping off 2 cubes at a time and writing the calculation.

$$14 - 2 = 12$$
$$12 - 2 = 10$$

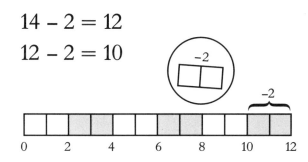

2 Keep making links from multiplication to division. *"If you know 6 lots of 2 makes 12, how many will there be in each group if you share out 12 equally into 2 groups?"*

3 Using number lines from Resource sheet 21, let the children draw hops of 2 and 10. *"Start on 30 and take hops of 10. How many hops back does it take to get to 0?"* (Grouping problems are best done on a number line.)

4 Work with the children to make the links from tables to division, using number lines whenever possible. *"If I know that 2 lots of 4 is 8, tell me a division fact I can work out."*

5 On a day when you are focusing on division by sharing equally, make sure the children can follow instructions, such as *"Divide these sweets into 2 (or 3 or 4) equal groups,"* and can at least share out using a '1 for you, 1 for me' strategy.

Teacher-independent activities

Choose from:

1 When the children are ready, they can complete Resource sheet 59 making equal hops back and recording the repeated subtractions.

2 Let the children use the Unifix number line independently. (See the adult-supported activities.) Ask them to set out a line of different colour cubes to take to the plenary session. For example, they can make a line of cubes to 24 with pairs in different colours so that they can demonstrate a repeated subtraction counting back in 2's from 24 to 0.

Plenary session

■ *"Show us your line of cubes and how you can count back in 2's."*

■ *"When we do repeated subtraction like this, what is the other operation sign we can use?"* (Division)

■ *"We can do division by repeated subtraction, but what is the opposite of doing repeated subtraction and what was the other sign we used then?"* (Multiplication)

■ *"When we are dividing things into 2's, would we have one left over if we started with an odd number? Will that happen with even numbers?"*

Money

Overall learning objectives

- To understand the relationship between all coins to £2.
- To be able to solve simple money problems.
- To begin to write money amounts including pounds.

> **Key words**
>
> | | | |
> |---|---|---|
> | coin | price | spend |
> | worth the most | cost | spent |
> | | buy | how much? |
> | pence | sell | total |
> | pound | bought | change |
> | £ | sold | |

Coin recognition

Assessment focus

- Can the children recognise all the coins up to £2?

Resources

- enough 1p, 2p, 5p, 10p, 20p, 50p, £1 and £2 coins so children can have one set between two
- giant copies of coins (such as Mega Money from BEAM)
- a bag
- Resource sheet 60
- a dice/spinner
- counters

With the whole class

- Give pairs of children the sets of coins and say *"Today you will be learning about all the coins, so talk about them first with your partner."* Ask *"Which is the biggest/smallest/lightest/heaviest? What colour are*

they? Which is worth the most/least? How do we know?" Hold up a 1p and ask the children to hold their 1p coins up. Ask what they are like. Repeat for all the other coins in order.

- Play 'What's My Coin?'. Say *"I'm thinking of a coin and it is silver and small. Guess my coin."* Repeat this a few times with various coins.

- Have a bag with one of each coin in. Choose a child to come to the front and select a coin by feel. Tell the child to use full sentences to describe the coin to the rest of the class, and ask the others to guess what the coin is, holding up the right one from their set. Repeat this.

With the lower-achievers

With adult support

Choose from:

1. Recap on the various denominations of coins. *"Which is worth the most/least? Which is the biggest/smallest?"*

2. Play 'What's My Coin?' again.

3. Ask individuals to hold up a specific coin to assess who needs more help with coin recognition. Ask any children who need more help to draw around each coin and write its value, or use Resource sheet 60 to match coins to the prices of the items shown.

Teacher-independent activities

Choose from:

1. Give pairs of children copies of Resource sheet 60 to play a matching game. Using another copy of the sheet, make a spinner from the diagram in the centre of the sheet (see page 4). Let the children take turns to spin the spinner and cover the corresponding item on the page with a counter. (So, for £2 they can cover the kite.) The first child to cover all the items correctly wins. (Encourage them to verbalise each time, for example *"I have got a 20p coin."*)

2. Let groups of two to four children use the border of Resource sheet 60 to play a game. Give them each a different colour counter, and ask them to take turns to spin the spinner and cover a matching coin with one of their

counters. The winner is the player who has the most counters on the border at the end of the game.

- Use the border of Resource sheet 60 for a race game with a 1–6 dice. Give the children a pot of coins. Tell them to start at the bottom left of the coin track, take turns to throw the dice and then move that many coins around the border. Explain that each time they land on a coin, they should take a matching one from the pot. The winner is the first child to reach the end of the track. Ask them to keep all the coins for the plenary session (when you can ask them to name them).

Plenary session

- *"Which coin is small and silver?"*
- *"Which coin is worth the least?"*
- *"I'm thinking of a coin and it is…"*
- *"Does anyone want more help with naming each coin?"*

Ordering coins

Assessment focus

- Can the children order coins?

Resources

- giant coins
- a washing line and pegs
- Resource sheets 61 and 68
- a set of coins for each child

With the whole class

- *"Today we are going to make a line of coins, starting with the one that is worth the least amount, and going all the way up in order to the one that can buy the most."*
- Ask the children to help you order the giant money on the line. Leave this on display.

- Make sure the children can name the coins and can say how much they are worth. More experienced children might be able to tell you how much more a coin is worth than the one before.

With the lower-achievers

With adult support

Choose from:

1 Repeat the starter activity. Ask the children to close their eyes while you put coins out of order. Then invite them to reorder them.

2 Use real coins to recap on recognising and describing each one. Ask each individual child to order a set of coins.

Teacher-independent activities

Choose from:

1 Give children copies of Resource sheet 61 and invite them to match coins (real if possible) to the coins on the top part of the sheet. Then ask them to join the coins in order, using the washing line as a guide. The lower part of the sheet asks them to find the right coins to 'buy' the various items. They can then join the items in order of cost in the same way.

2 Use Resource sheet 68 (money clip art) to make a similar sheet, pricing various toys and so on to join in order of cost.

3 Enlarge the pictures from Resource sheet 68, write some prices by the items and ask the children to match the correct coins to them and put them in order of value.

Plenary session

- Order coins again, emphasising 'worth the least/most'.
- *"Would I have more money if I had this coin,"* (holding up 1p) *"or this coin?"* (holding up £1)
- *"A balloon costs 5p. Would I have enough to buy one with this coin?"* (Hold up 10p.) *"Could I buy more than one?"*

Exchanging

Assessment focus

- Can the children exchange coins?

Resources

- a large sheet of paper and marker pen
- coins
- 1–6 dice
- a abacus, place value board and cards
- number cards
- Resource sheet 62

With the whole class

- It would be useful to repeat some of the earlier work with place value cards so that the children will make links between what they already know and what you are teaching.

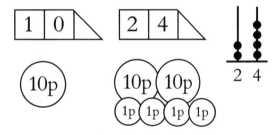

Make links to place value.

- Draw a diagram (see below) on a large sheet of paper to demonstrate how when we have 10

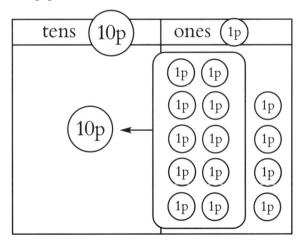

pennies we can exchange them for a 10p coin. Place a 10p coin in the appropriate column. Demonstrate this on an abacus and with place value cards, showing the 0 holding the place in the units column.

- Add pennies one at a time to make 14p, talking about what you are doing. Continue adding coins until you get to 20p, show another exchange with a second 10p coin and then go on adding pennies again.

With the lower-achievers

With adult support

Choose from:

1 Go on adding one or more pennies at a time to the large diagram you drew in the whole-class starter session, exchanging for 10p coins as necessary.

2 Ask the children to each take a handful of pennies. Remind them of what we do when we are counting lots of things. Remind them that we can count in 2's to make piles of 10. Then ask what they could do with the piles of 10 pennies. Encourage the response that they could exchange the pennies for a 10p coin.

Teacher-independent activities

Choose from:

1 Give the children each a copy of Resource sheet 62, and ask them to play in pairs or small groups. Tell them to take turns to throw the 1–6 dice and take the appropriate amount of 1p coins, placing them in the 1p column. Explain that when a player has 10 or more pennies, 10 of them should be exchanged for one 10p coin, which is then put in the 10p column. (Be aware that once they have one 10p coin, children often start to pick up 10p coins instead of pennies at their next throw of the dice. Make sure they know that the dice number always refers to the number of pennies.) Tell them that when they have one 10p and some pennies, they will be able to 'buy' toys by putting the correct amounts of money onto the pictures at the bottom of the sheet. So, for example, if they have 12p they can 'buy' the rubber ring.

2 Ask the children to lay out corresponding amounts of money in order next to some number cards. This will help to reinforce the 'teen' numbers for those that need that support.

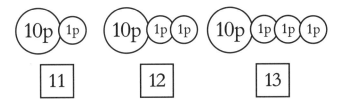

Plenary session

■ Let the children demonstrate exchanges, focusing on their language as they describe what they are doing.

■ Make links to an abacus.

Money maths

Assessment focus

■ Can the children make amounts up to 10p, 20p, 50p and £1 (and exchange coins)?

Resources

■ a large pot or purse of real 1p and 10p coins

■ a place value board and cards

■ a 1p/10p spinner

■ 1–6 dice

■ Resource sheets 6, 62, 63, 64, 65 and 68

■ counters

With the whole class

■ Begin by saying *"Today we are going to learn about why we have lots of different kinds of coins."* Show the children a large number of 1p coins and point out how heavy they are and what it would be like to go to a shop to buy something expensive like a bike and have to pay for it all in 1p coins! We would end up with holes in our pockets from the weight!

■ Say *"Ten 1p's are worth the same as one 10p."* Relate this to using a place value board and cards.

■ Count out 1p coins up to 10p. Ask what can be done when we reach 10 pennies (exchange for a 10p coin and put it in the 10p column). Go on to count the coins onwards from the 10p, and demonstrate how to write these amounts. Remind the children of the place value move to the left.

■ Put out another amount of pennies above 10 and ask a child to count them. Prompt the child to exchange 10 pennies for a 10p coin. Let the child write the amount on the board. Repeat this a few times with other children.

■ Ask *"If 10 pennies go together to make a 10p coin, how many do you think go together to make 5p, 20p and 50p coins?"*

■ Count 10p coins together. *"1 ten, 2 tens, 3 tens... These are just like the multiples of 10."* Count them again. *"10p, 20p, 30p..."* and so on up to 80p. Demonstrate how to write these amounts.

■ Put out ten 10p coins, and say *"Ten 10p coins are worth £1."* Show the children a £1 coin and make the exchange. Demonstrate how to write £1.00, pointing out that there is one pound but no 10p's or 1p's, therefore we write £1.00. Count out twelve 10p's and show them how to write this as pence – 120p. Tell them that you are going to exchange ten 10p's for a £1 coin and show them how to write that – 100p. Invite the children to take turns to write other amounts.

With the lower-achievers

With adult support

Choose from:

1 Recap on how many 1p's there are in 10p. Give the group a pot of 1p coins. Let them take turns to throw a dice and then take the corresponding amount of 1p coins. After three goes, ask them to count their coins. If they have 10 pennies or more, give them 10p coins in exchange. Then ask them to write down how much they have. The one with the most money wins.

2 Play the same game using 10p coins. Begin by recapping on how many 10p's there are in £1.

3   Recap on how many 1p's there are in 10p and how many 10ps there are in £1. Then play the game again using both denominations and a 1p/10p spinner.

4   Ask individuals to make specific amounts just with 10p and 1p coins so that you can assess understanding. *"Sofie, you make 21p, and Gus, you make 34p."*

Teacher-independent activities

Choose from:

1   Let the children play the game on Resource sheet 62 again but with new pictures from the money clip art on Resource sheet 68, maybe moving some children on to larger amounts if appropriate.

2   Fill in Resource sheet 63 with amounts suitable for your children, then ask them to work individually to add up and write the amounts.

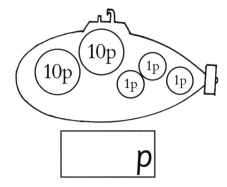

3   Let the children work with Resource sheet 64, matching the amounts to the number lines.

4   Let the children work with a partner to play a money trail game made from Resource sheet 6. Each pair will need a 1–6 dice, counters and a pot of pennies. Explain that if they land on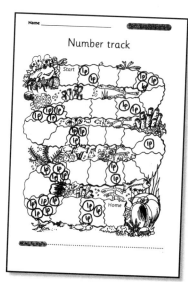

a coin space they should take the amount of money shown. The winner is the one with the most when they reach the end. You could vary the game by using 10p coins as well.

5   Give the children copies of Resource sheet 65 to complete. The 10's and 1's are laid out like place value cards, which will support this activity.

Plenary session

- *"How many 10p's in 20p?"*
- *"Come and make up 14 pence, Dan."*
- *"How many 1p's in 50p?"*

Shopping

Assessment focus

- Can the children solve simple shopping problems with amounts of money up to £1?

Resources

- a large number line and '+' and '–' operation cards
- dice
- counters
- 10p and 1p coins
- Resource sheets 6, 66 and 68

With the whole class

- Begin by saying *"We will be working on shopping problems today. Joe had 8p and his mum gave him 10p, so how much has he got now?"* Show the children how to add 10 on a large number line and show them an addition operation card. Say *"Sarah had 20p. She spent 5p on sweets and 10p on a comic, so how much has she got left?"* Show the subtraction operation card and demonstrate how you can solve this by either counting back or counting on along the number line.

- Offer more problems, such as *"Tim got 50p pocket money and earned 30p for washing up. He spent half* of it on sweets, so how much has he got left?" Ask the children what sort of calculation each question is and how they worked out the answer. Ask them to demonstrate on the number line how they could work it out and hold up the appropriate operation card.

■ Say "It is important to be able to work out how much change you should have when spending money." Recap on how many 1p's there are in 5p, 10p, 20p, 50p and £1, and how many 10p's there are in 20p, 50p and £1.

■ Say "Jackie had £1 and spent 20p on crisps and 30p on an ice cream. How much change did she get? Ramu had 20p and bought a chocolate bar for 17p. How much change did he have?"

With the lower-achievers

With adult support
Choose from:

1 Use Resource sheet 6 to make a shopping game as shown below. Fill it in with amounts the children win in circles and the amounts they spend in squares. Let each child start with two 10p coins and five 1p coins. Act as 'banker' yourself with a pot of coins. Explain that they must take turns to throw the dice and move a counter along the trail. If they land on a circle they get the amount of money, but if they land on a square they have to spend that amount of

money. If a child runs out of money they are out of the game. When the first child reaches the end of the trail, everyone should count up their money, swapping 1p coins for 10p coins if appropriate. The player with the most money wins.

2 Set simple problems with as many different coins as your children can manage, for example "Jack has 10p and spends 7p, so how much is left?" Ask questions individually where you can so that you can assess progress. Give children number lines if appropriate and show each child how to count out change accurately.

Teacher-independent activities
Choose from:

1 Adapt Resource sheet 6 to make a shopping game in pairs, making it as complex as children can cope with on their own. You could have a more experienced child working with them as the 'banker'.

2 Give children copies of Resource sheet 66, and ask them to draw around the coins they need to make up the amounts on the pictures. You can make a more complex or an easier sheet using the money clip art from Resource sheet 68.

Plenary session

■ "If I have 10p and spend 6p on sweets, how much will I have left?"

■ "If an apple costs 5p, how much do I need to buy three of them?"

■ "Tell me one way I could make 8 pence. Can you think of another way?"

0	1	2
3	4	5
6	7	8
9	10	11

12	13	14
15	16	17
18	19	20

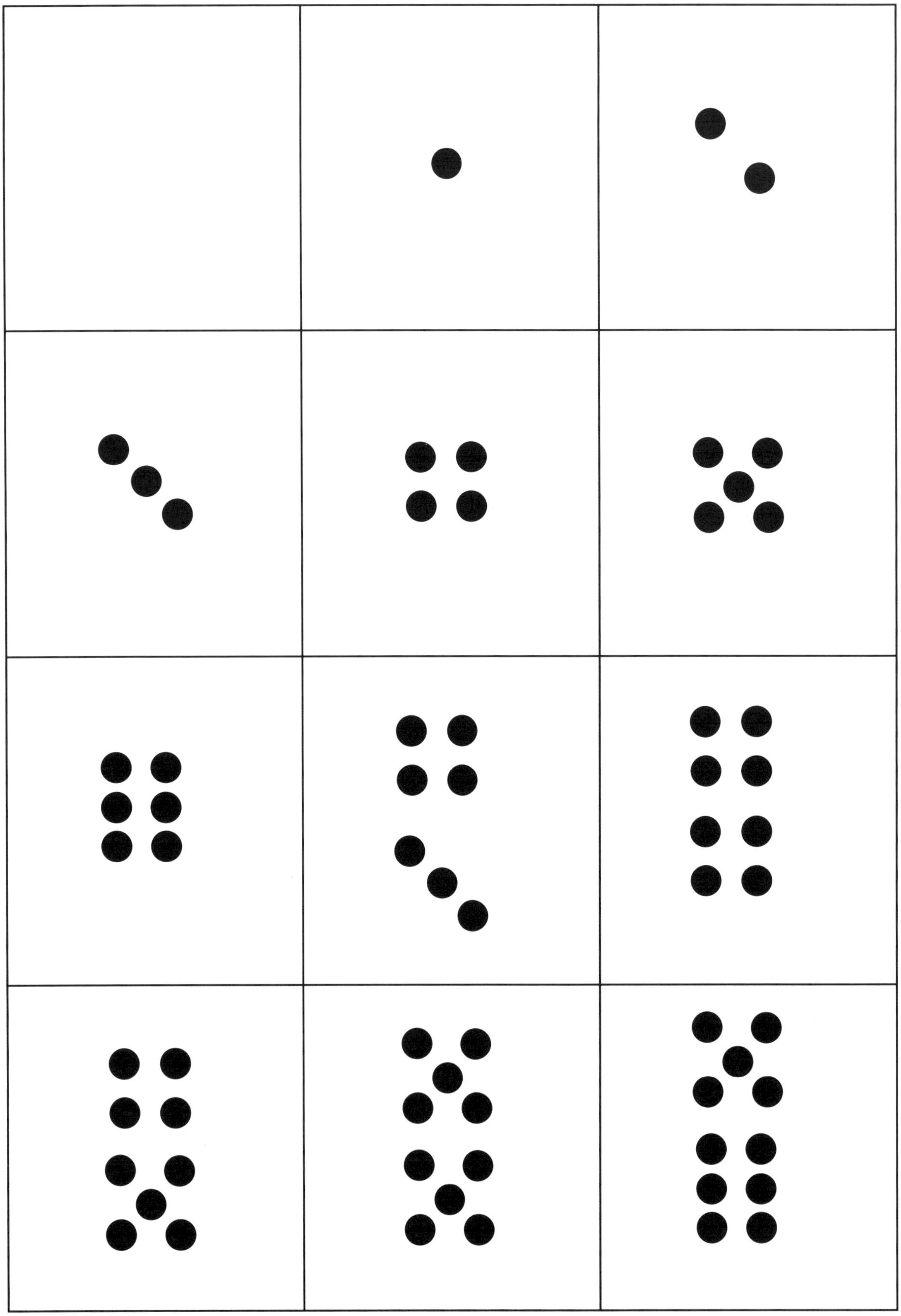

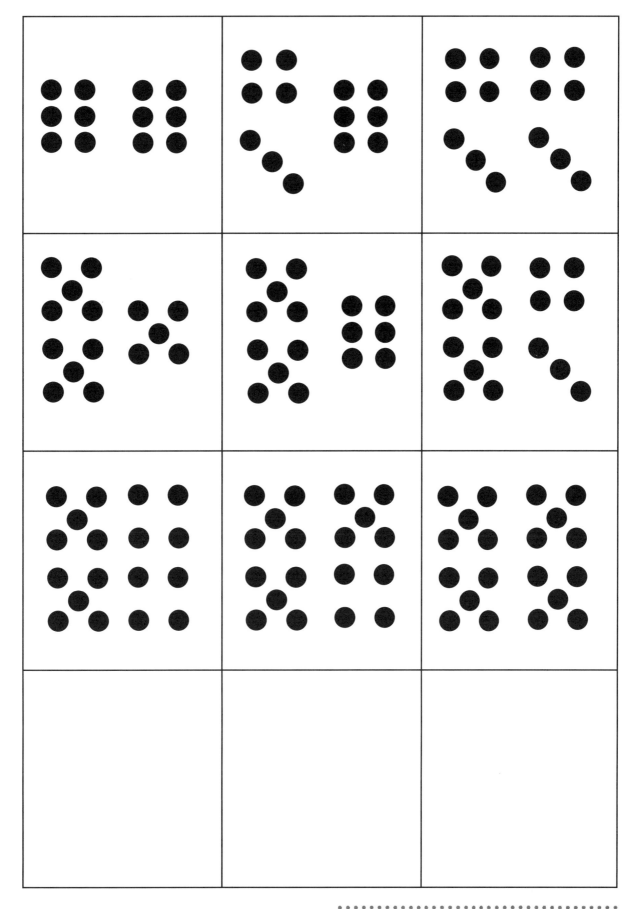

Fish game

Number track

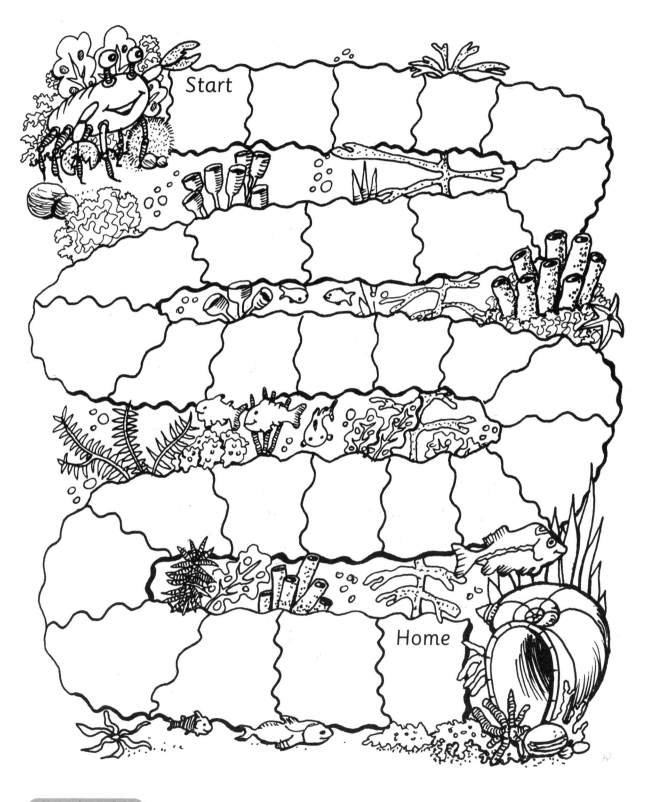

Start

Home

Bingo cards

Name _____

Number lines

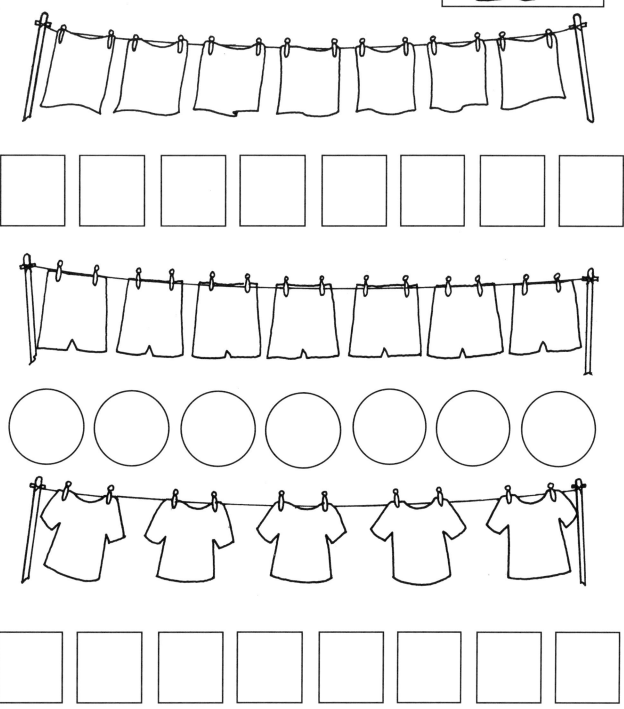

100 square

1	2	3	4	5	6	7	8	9	10
11	12	13	14	15	16	17	18	19	20
21	22	23	24	25	26	27	28	29	30
31	32	33	34	35	36	37	38	39	40
41	42	43	44	45	46	47	48	49	50
51	52	53	54	55	56	57	58	59	60
61	62	63	64	65	66	67	68	69	70
71	72	73	74	75	76	77	78	79	80
81	82	83	84	85	86	87	88	89	90
91	92	93	94	95	96	97	98	99	100

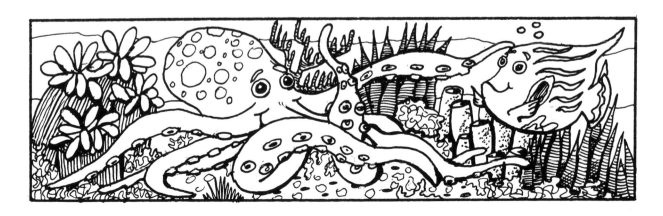

Blank 100 square

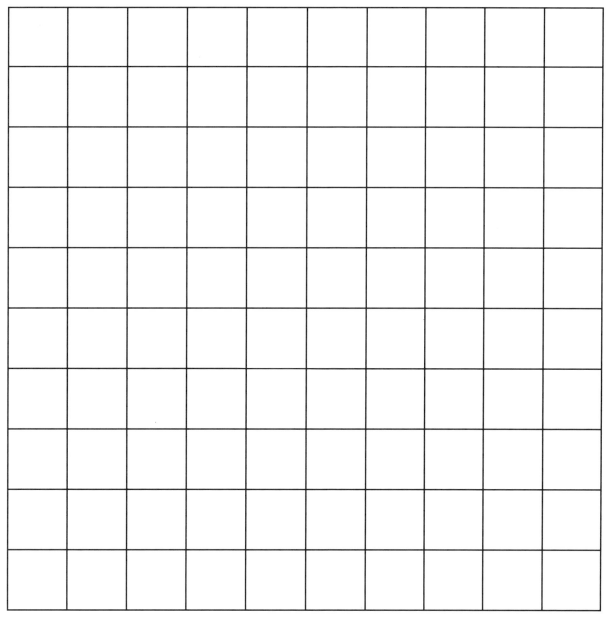

Making patterns

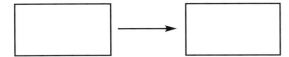

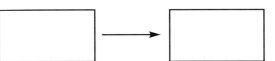

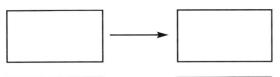

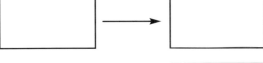

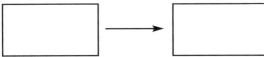

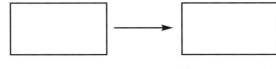

Notes for adults •

• •

Three in a row

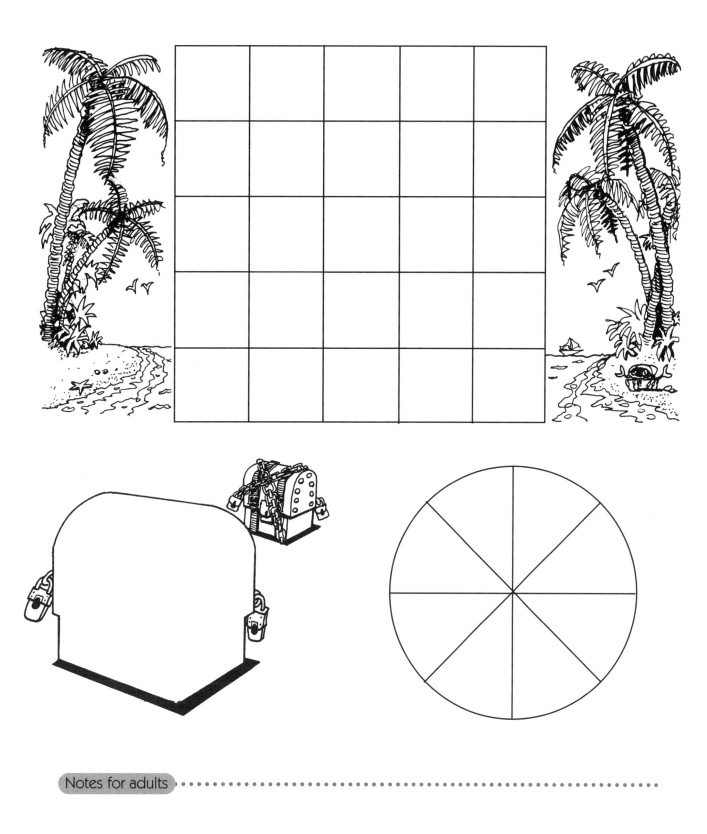

Snake race

Less than, more than

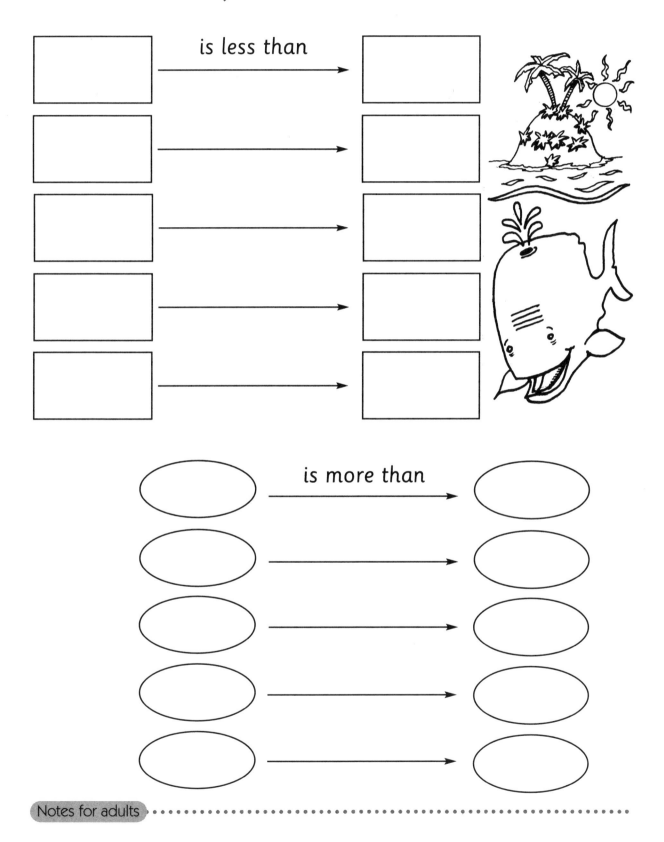

is less than

is more than

Greater than

Circle the greater number in each pair.

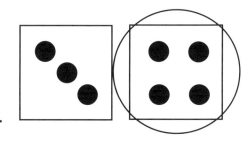

1.

6   7

2.
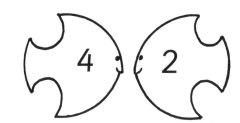
4   2

3.
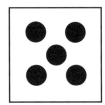 

4.

17   18

5.

10   12

6.
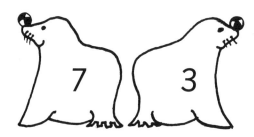
7   3

7.

10   7

8.

22   19

9.
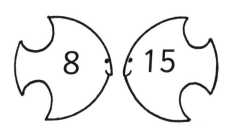
8   15

10.
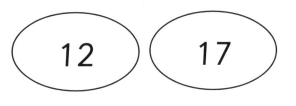
12   17

Write numbers greater than 20.

10's and 1's

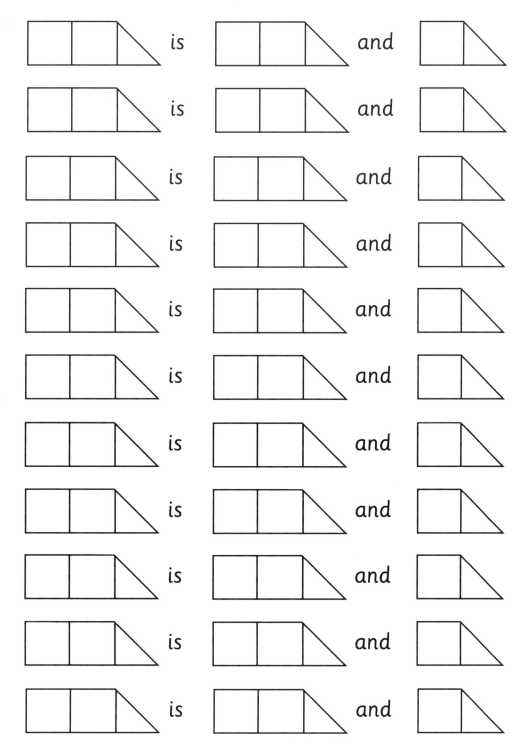

is   and

is   and

is   and

is   and

is   and

is   and

is   and

is   and

is   and

is   and

is   and

Split up

Split up 10

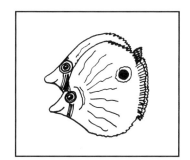

☐   ☐☐☐☐☐☐☐☐☐

1   and   9 $1 + 9 = 10$

☐☐   ☐☐☐☐☐☐☐☐

2   and   8 $2 + 8 = 10$

Notes for adults •

Help the children to work systematically.

Split up ☐

Notes for adults •

The children should make a cube 'train' of 8 or 15 or 20, for example, then split it into two parts, for example 8 is 1 + 7. Once they have chosen a number to work with they must keep to that number.
• •

Join pairs to make ☐

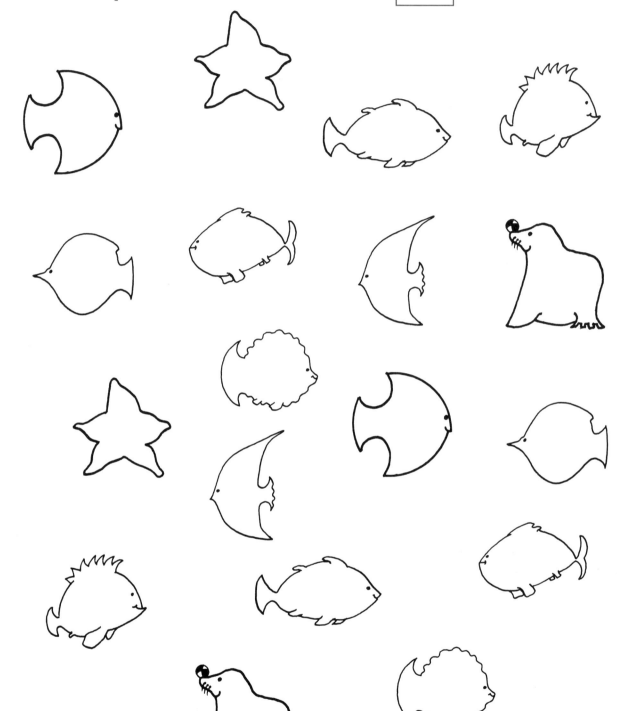

Name _____

Draw more to make ☐

5 flags. Draw ☐ more.

2 faces. Draw ☐ more.

6 circles. Draw ☐ more.

4 worms. Draw ☐ more.

7 squares. Draw ☐ more.

3 balls. Draw ☐ more.

8 lollies. Draw ☐ more.

9 crabs. Draw ☐ more.

Number line/track

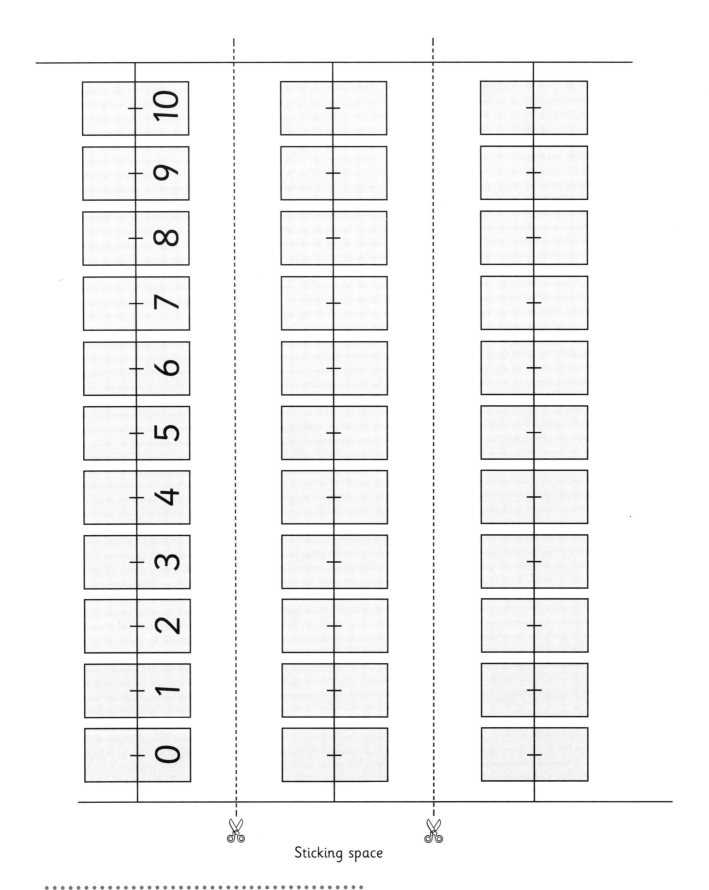

Sticking space

Counting on

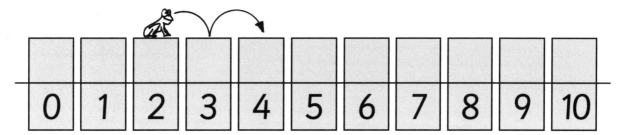

2 + 2 = ☐

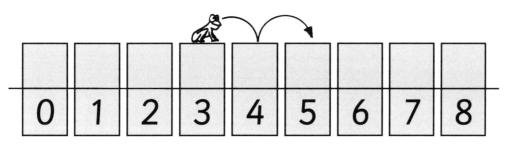

3 + 4 = ☐

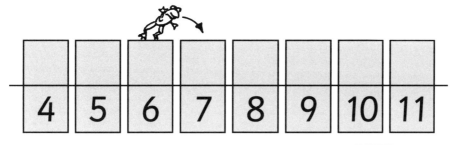

6 + 3 = ☐

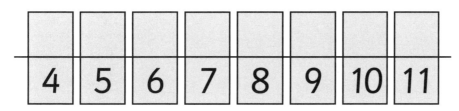

☐ + ☐ = ☐

Notes for adults ••

Make sure children make 'hops' with fingers first. Then draw in their hops.

Frog hops

1.

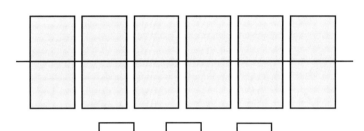

☐ + ☐ = ☐

2.

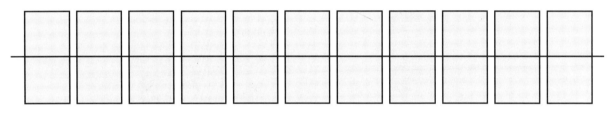

☐ + ☐ = ☐

3.

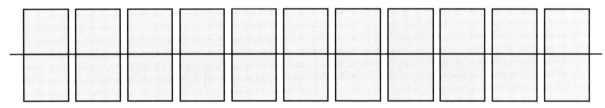

☐ + ☐ = ☐

4.

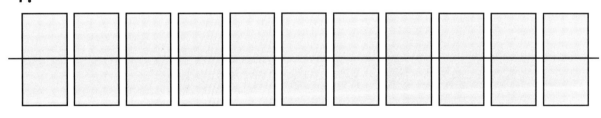

☐ + ☐ = ☐

Notes for adults •

• •

Addition

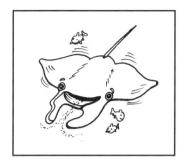

☐ + ☐ = ☐   ☐ + ☐ = ☐

☐ + ☐ = ☐   ☐ + ☐ = ☐

☐ + ☐ = ☐   ☐ + ☐ = ☐

☐ + ☐ = ☐   ☐ + ☐ = ☐

☐ + ☐ = ☐   ☐ + ☐ = ☐

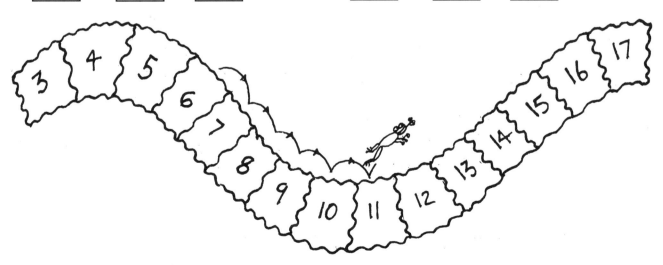

Notes for adults ●

Help the children to take 'steps' along a number line or track.

Adding

 add = ☐

2   +   4   = ☐

2   +   4   = ☐   4   +   2   = ☐

6   +   2   = ☐   3   +   3   = ☐

9   +   3   = ☐   7   +   4   = ☐

Notes for adults •

Make more sheets, replacing the picture at the top with another from the clip art pictures on Resource sheet 69 (page 126).

• •

82

Change it around

2 + 4 ⟳⟶ 4 + 2 = ☐

☐ + ⟳⟶ ☐ + = ☐

☐ + ⟳⟶ ☐ + = ☐

☐ + ⟳⟶ ☐ + = ☐

☐ + ⟳⟶ ☐ + = ☐

☐ + ⟳⟶ ☐ + = ☐

☐ + ⟳⟶ ☐ + = ☐

☐ + ⟳⟶ ☐ + = ☐

Notes for adults •••

Make 10

1.

$$5 + 5 + 2$$

$$10 + 2 = \boxed{}$$

2.

$$7 + 2 + 3$$

$$\boxed{} + 2 = \boxed{}$$

3.

$$6 + 4 + 1$$

$$\boxed{} + 1 = \boxed{}$$

4.

$$9 + 5 + 1$$

$$\boxed{} + 5 = \boxed{}$$

5.

$$8 + 3 + 2$$

$$10 + \boxed{} = \boxed{}$$

6.

$$4 + 3 + 6$$

$$\boxed{} + \boxed{} = \boxed{}$$

7.

$$3 + 4 + 7$$

$$\boxed{} + \boxed{} = \boxed{}$$

Notes for adults •

Help the children to identify the pairs of numbers that make 10.
The two numbers could be circled in colour first.

• •

Name _____

Number lines

$3 + 10 = 13$ +10
3   13

1.

[   ] _____ = [   ]

2.

[   ] _____ = [   ]

3.

[   ] _____ = [   ]

4.

[   ] _____ = [   ]

5.

[   ] _____ = [   ]

Notes for adults •

Help the children to draw their 'hops' along the number lines and to write the calculations.

Dice game

Seashore game

Name _____

Hopping back

1.

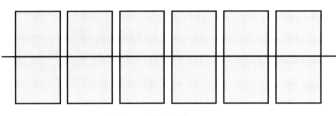

☐ – ☐ = ☐

2.

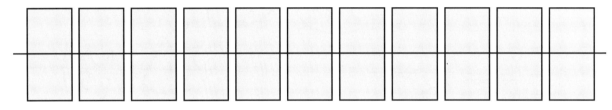

☐ – ☐ = ☐

3.

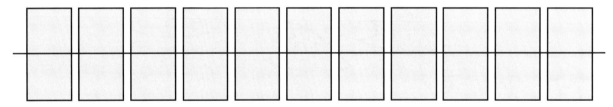

☐ – ☐ = ☐

4.

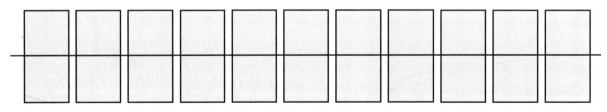

☐ – ☐ = ☐

Notes for adults ●

● ●

Counting back

1.

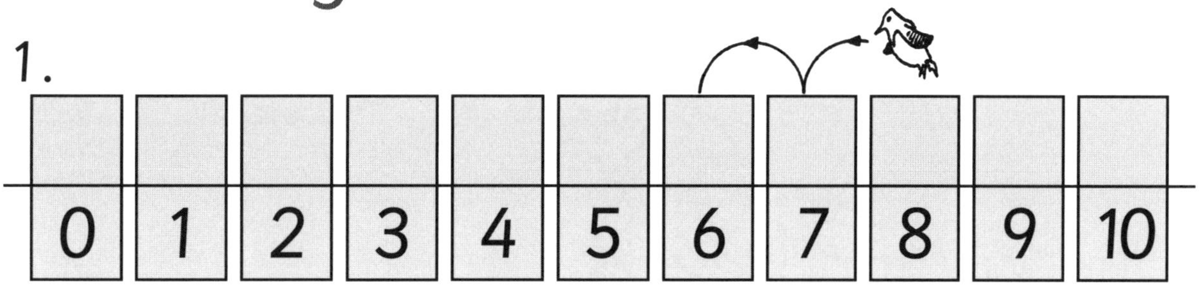

| 0 | 1 | 2 | 3 | 4 | 5 | 6 | 7 | 8 | 9 | 10 |

8 – 2 = ☐

2.

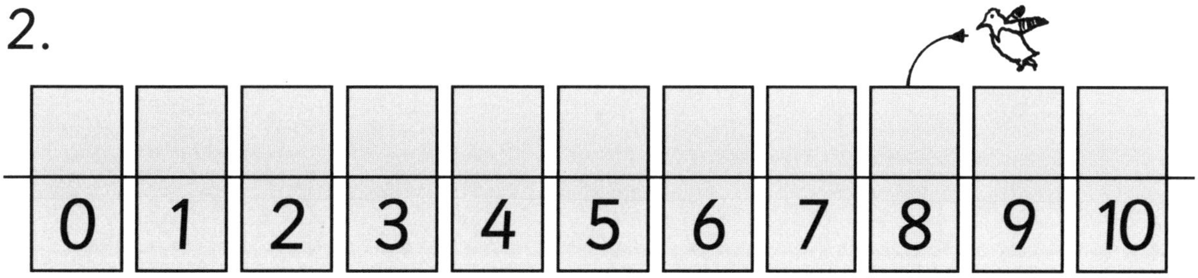

| 0 | 1 | 2 | 3 | 4 | 5 | 6 | 7 | 8 | 9 | 10 |

9 – 2 = ☐

3.

| 0 | 1 | 2 | 3 | 4 | 5 | 6 | 7 | 8 | 9 | 10 |

7 – 2 = ☐

4.

| 0 | 1 | 2 | 3 | 4 | 5 | 6 | 7 | 8 | 9 | 10 |

☐ – ☐ = ☐

Notes for adults ••

Name _____

Subtractions

5 6 7 8 9 10 11 12 13 14 15 16 17 18 19 20

☐ – ☐ = ☐   ☐ – ☐ = ☐

☐ – ☐ = ☐   ☐ – ☐ = ☐

☐ – ☐ = ☐   ☐ – ☐ = ☐

☐ – ☐ = ☐   ☐ – ☐ = ☐

☐ – ☐ = ☐   ☐ – ☐ = ☐

☐ – ☐ = ☐   ☐ – ☐ = ☐

Notes for adults •••

Help the children to take 'steps' along a number line or track.

90

Number line subtraction

$17 - 10 = 7$

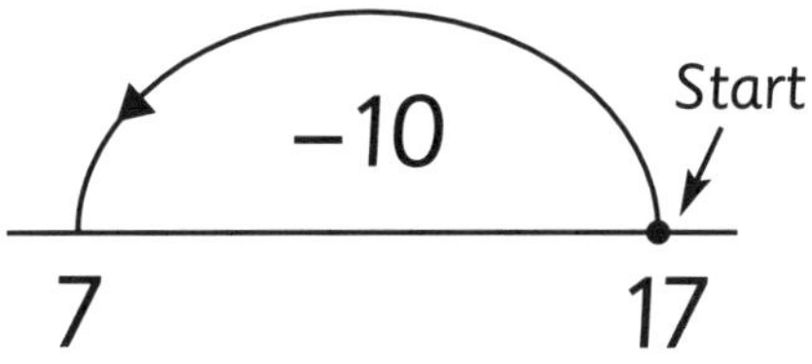

−10   Start

7   17

1.

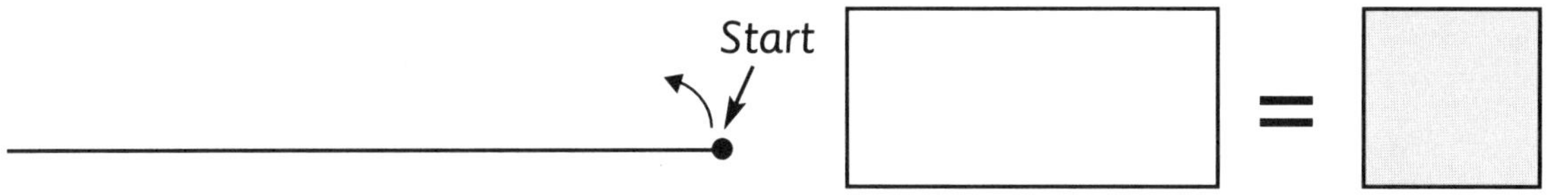

Start

[   ] = [   ]

2.

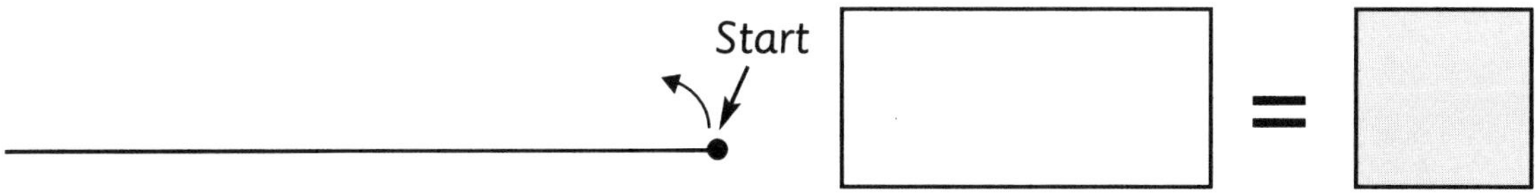

Start

[   ] = [   ]

3.

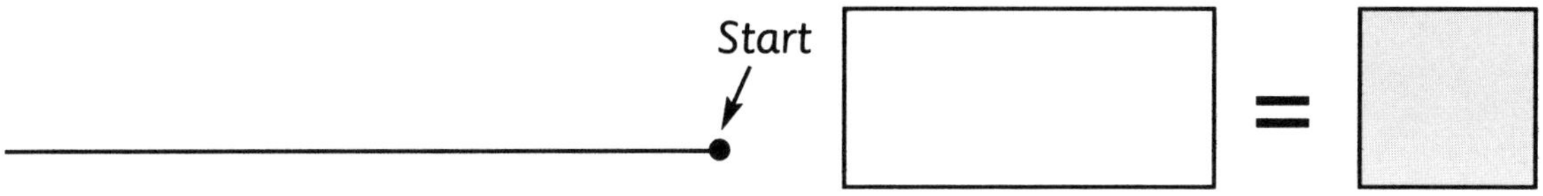

Start

[   ] = [   ]

4.

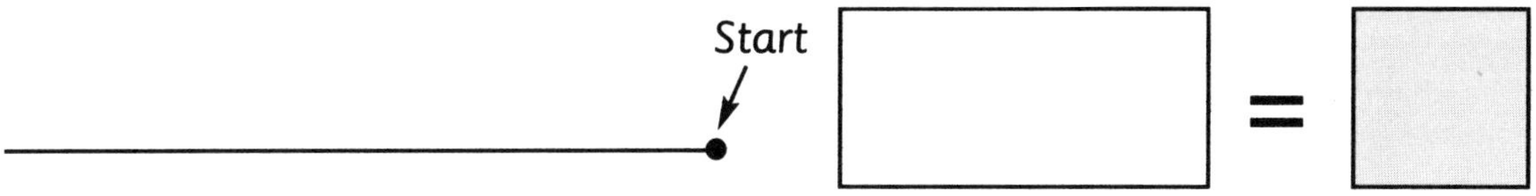

Start

[   ] = [   ]

5.

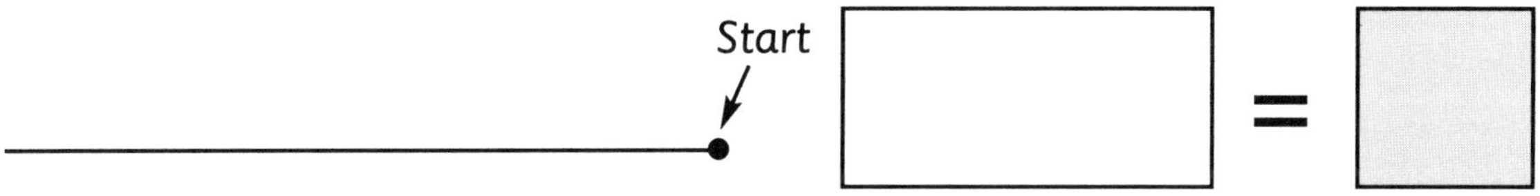

Start

[   ] = [   ]

Notes for adults •

Help the children to start at the right-hand side of the line.

Take away

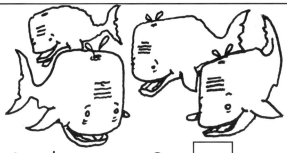

4 take away 2 = ☐

5 take away 3 = ☐

7 take away 1 = ☐

6 take away 2 = ☐

5 take away 4 = ☐

7 take away 2 = ☐

8 take away 4 = ☐

7 take away 5 = ☐

Notes for adults •

Crossing out

4 cross out 1 = ☐

6 cross out ☐ = ☐

3 cross out ☐ = ☐

7 cross out ☐ = ☐

5 cross out ☐ = ☐

☐ cross out ☐ = ☐

☐ cross out ☐ = ☐

☐ cross out ☐ = ☐

Notes for adults •

How many are hiding?

[   ] fish in each chest.

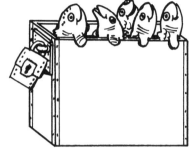
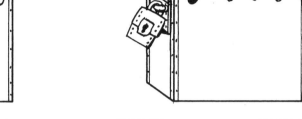

[   ] fish   [   ] hiding   [   ] fish   [   ] hiding

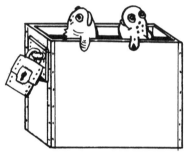
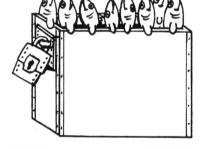

[   ] fish   [   ] hiding   [   ] fish   [   ] hiding

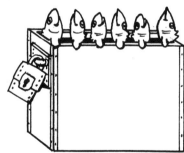
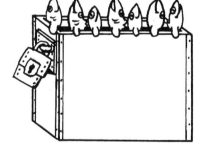

[   ] fish   [   ] hiding   [   ] fish   [   ] hiding

Notes for adults •

Use counters under a cloth for this activity.

• •

Name _____

Secret numbers

$3 +$  $= 6$

$4 +$ ☐ $= 7$

$5 +$ ⬭ $= 10$

$4 +$ 🐟 $= 8$

☐ $=$ ◯ $+$ ◯   ☐ $-$ ☐ $=$ ☐

☐ $=$ 🐟 $+$ 🐟   ◯ $-$ ◯ $=$ ◯

☐ $=$ ☐ $+$ ☐   🐟 $-$ 🐟 $=$ ◯

☐ $=$ ◯ $+$ ◯   ◯ $-$ ◯ $=$ ◯

What's the difference?

5 ⭐ ⭐ ⭐ ⭐ ⭐

3 ⭐ ⭐ ⭐

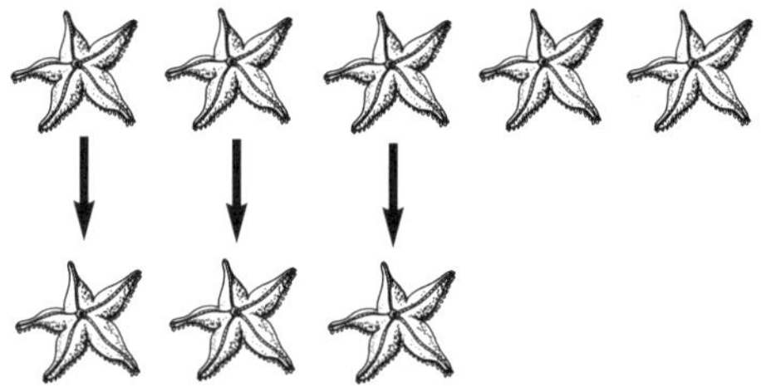

Difference is ☐

7 🐟 🐟 🐟 🐟 🐟 🐟 🐟

4 🐟 🐟 🐟 🐟

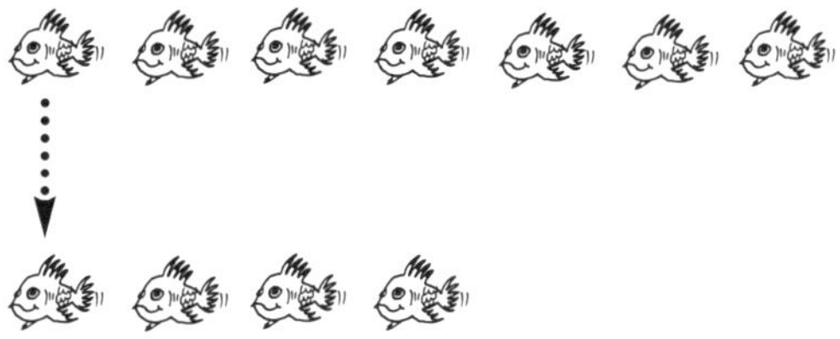

Difference is ☐

6 🐟 🐟 🐟 🐟 🐟 🐟

2 🐟 🐟

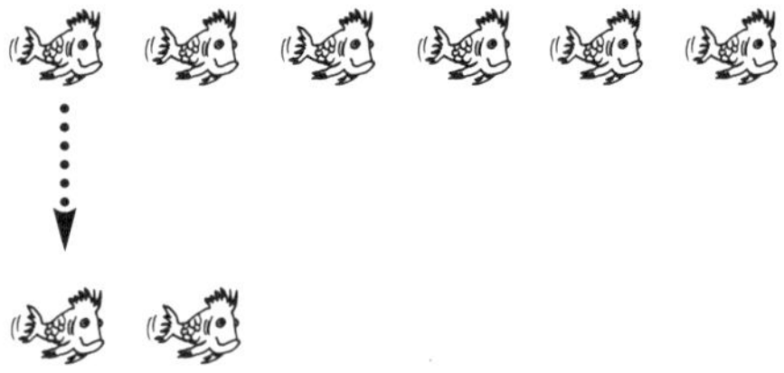

Difference is ☐

5 ☐ ☐ ☐ ☐ ☐

6 ☐ ☐ ☐ ☐ ☐ ☐

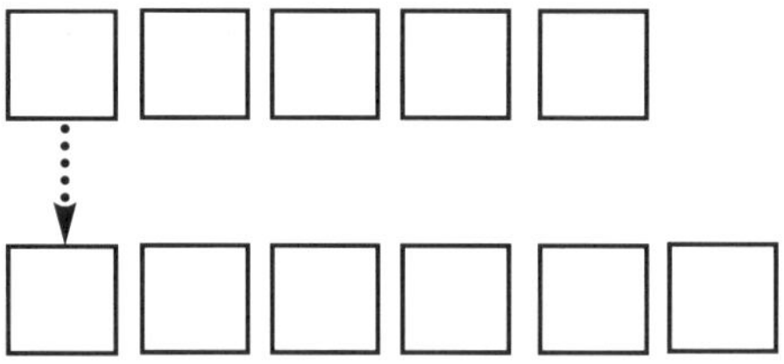

Difference is ☐

8 ● ● ● ● ● ● ● ●

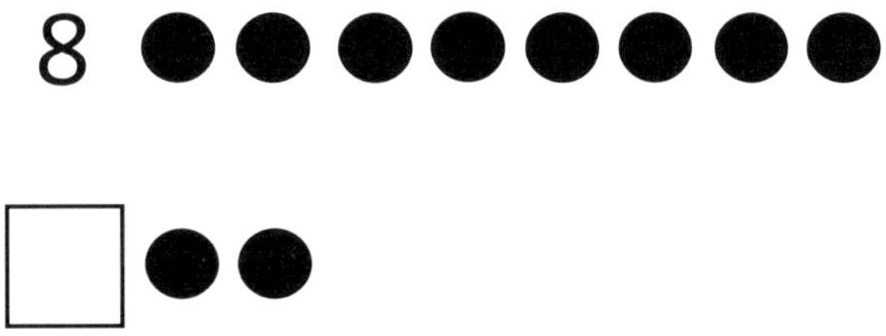

☐ ● ●

Difference is ☐

7 ○ ○ ○ ○ ○ ○ ○

3 ○ ○ ○

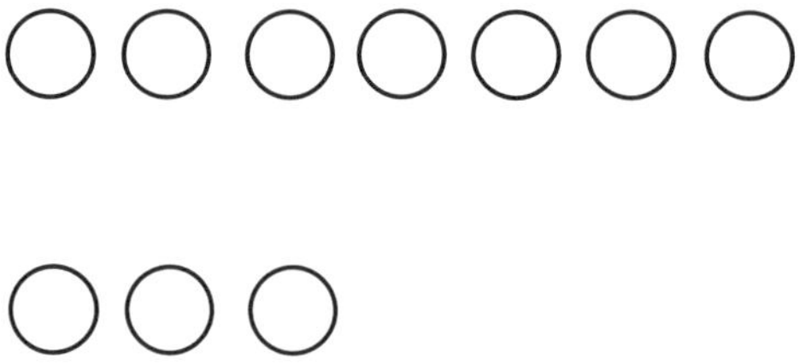

Difference is ☐

Difference is ☐

Difference is ☐

Name _____

It's the same number!

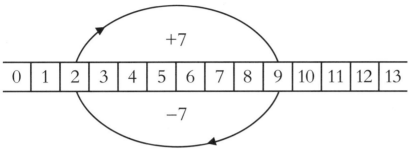

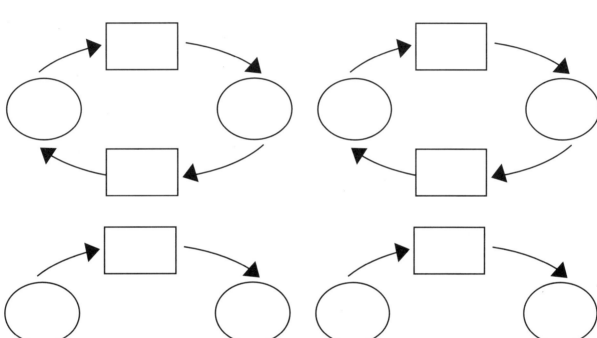

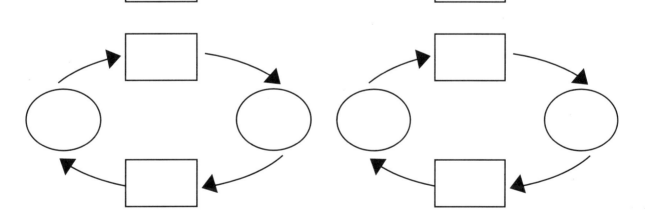

Notes for adults

Track game

Start

Doubles

double 1 is ☐   double 2 is ☐   double 3 is ☐

double ☐ is ☐   double ☐ is ☐   double ☐ is ☐

double ☐ is ☐   double ☐ is ☐   double ☐ is ☐

double ☐ is ☐   double ☐ is ☐   double ☐ is ☐

Notes for adults ●

The children have to draw some dots to make doubles.

● ●

Double add 1

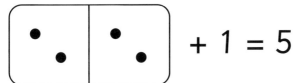 + 1 = 5

Write more here.

☐ + 1 = ☐

☐ + 1 = ☐

☐ + 1 = ☐

☐ + 1 = ☐

☐ + 1 = ☐

Notes for adults ●

The children should draw in double dots on the dominoes and add 1. After doing 6 + 6 + 1 they can go on to make more of their own, such as 7 + 7 + 1.

Double and halve

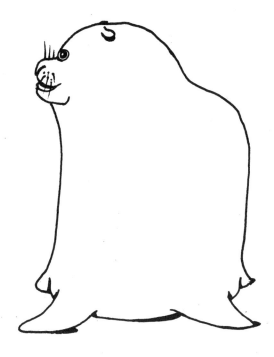 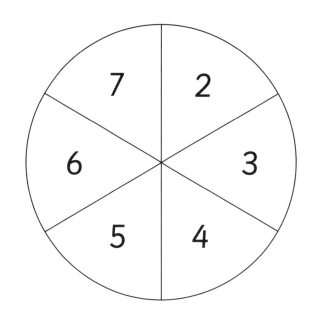

7   2
6   3
5   4

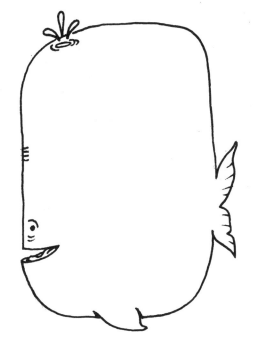 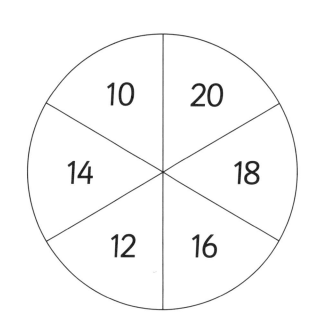

10   20
14   18
12   16

Name _____

Fingers

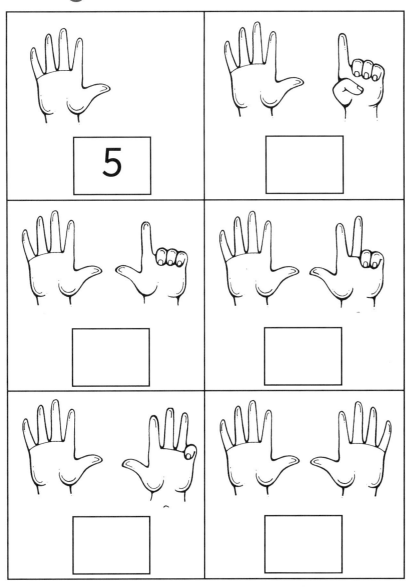

$5 + 5 = 10$

$5 + 6 = \Box$

$5 + 7 = \Box$

$5 + 8 = \Box$

$5 + 9 = \Box$

$5 + 10 = \Box$

Notes for adults ·

· ·
102

Tens and units

| 1 | 3 | + | 1 | 0 |

10 + 3 + 10 = 20 + 3 = 23

1. | 1 | 4 | + | 1 | 0 |

10 + 4 + 10 = 20 + ☐ = ☐

2. | 2 | 3 | + | 1 | 0 |

20 + 3 + ☐ = 30 + ☐ = ☐

3. | 1 | 5 | + | 1 | 1 |

10 + ☐ + ☐ + ☐ = ☐

4. | 1 | 6 | + | 1 | 2 |

☐ + ☐ + ☐ + ☐ = ☐

Notes for adults •

See also Resource sheet 16. Work with the children using place value cards.

• •
103

Name _____

Grids

+	0	1	2
1	1	2	3
2	2	3	4

■ Fill in the grids.

Name _____

Target

Fishy game

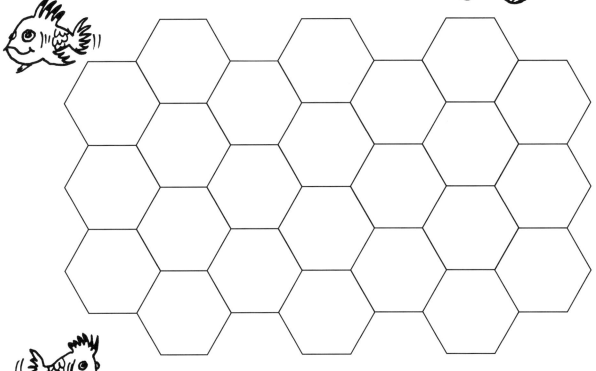

and	add	plus	+
makes	equals	altogether makes	
make	leaves	subtract	
minus	–	=	is
the difference between		cross out	
take away	count on	count back	

Cut out the words to make number sentences.

Magic 3 numbers

Use ☐ ☐ and ☐

☐ count on ☐ land on ☐

☐ add ☐ makes ☐

☐ add ☐ equals ☐

☐ take away ☐ = ☐

☐ count back ☐ land on ☐

☐ cross out ☐ leaves ☐

☐ = ☐ + ☐

Lots of

Today I'm using ☐ cubes.

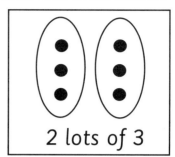

2 lots of 3

I can make

☐ lots of ☐

I can make

☐ lots of ☐

I can make

☐ lots of ☐

I can make

☐ lots of ☐

Notes for adults ···

Arrays

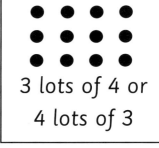

3 lots of 4 or
4 lots of 3

This is

☐ lots of ☐

☐ lots of ☐

This is

☐ lots of ☐

☐ lots of ☐

This is

☐ lots of ☐

☐ lots of ☐

Notes for adults ●

● ●

Name _____

Find pairs

■ Match the calculations.

6 x 2
3 lots of 4
8 lots of 2
5 lots of 2
10 lots of 2
6 lots of 3
9 x 2
10 lots of 10
8 lots of 3

2 + 2 + 2 + 2 + 2 + 2

2 + 2 + 2 + 2 + 2 + 2 + 2 + 2

4 + 4 + 4

3 + 3 + 3 + 3 + 3 + 3

2 + 2 + 2 + 2 + 2

2 + 2 + 2 + 2 + 2 + 2 + 2 + 2 + 2 + 2

3 + 3 + 3 + 3 + 3 + 3 + 3 + 3

2 + 2 + 2 + 2 + 2 + 2 + 2 + 2 + 2

10 + 10 + 10 + 10 + 10 + 10 + 10 + 10 + 10 + 10

Notes for adults ●

● ●

10 times game

* any number

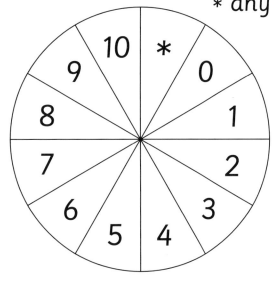

0 x 10 = ☐

1 x 10 = ☐

2 x 10 = ☐

3 x 10 = ☐

4 x 10 = ☐

5 x 10 = ☐

6 x 10 = ☐

7 x 10 = ☐

8 x 10 = ☐

9 x 10 = ☐

10 x 10 = ☐

Notes for adults ••• Resource sheet 55

••••••••••••••••••••••••••

2 times game

* any number

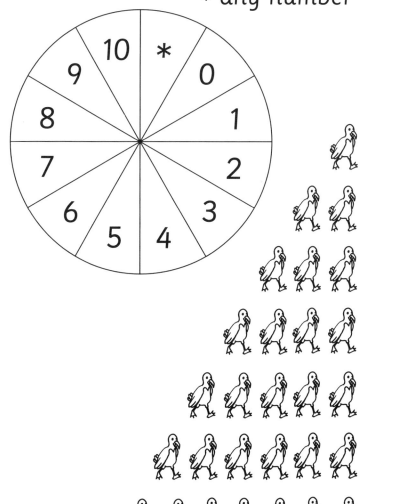

0 x 2 = ☐

1 x 2 = ☐

2 x 2 = ☐

3 x 2 = ☐

4 x 2 = ☐

5 x 2 = ☐

6 x 2 = ☐

7 x 2 = ☐

8 x 2 = ☐

9 x 2 = ☐

10 x 2 = ☐

Notes for adults •

• •

0 x 2	1 x 2
2 x 2	3 x 2
4 x 2	5 x 2
6 x 2	7 x 2
8 x 2	9 x 2
10 x 2	

0 x 10	1 x 10
2 x 10	3 x 10
4 x 10	5 x 10
6 x 10	7 x 10
8 x 10	9 x 10
10 x 10	

Repeated subtraction

−5   −5

0   5   10

$$10 - 5 - 5 = 0$$

1.

−2

12

$$12 - 2 \qquad\qquad = 0$$

2.

−2

10

$$10 - 2 \qquad\qquad = 0$$

3.

−3

15

$$15 - 3 \qquad\qquad = 0$$

4.

−4

12

$$12 - 4 \qquad\qquad = 0$$

Money game

Start

Finish

Notes for adults

The children have to spin the spinner (see page 4 for how to make it) and win that coin. They cover the items with the correct amount or cover the coins in the border. See the teachers' notes on pages 52 and 53.

Ordering money

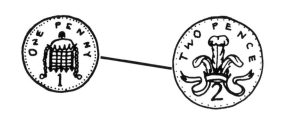

Notes for adults •

The children first join the money at the top of the sheet in order of value. They then put coins on the items for sale and join them in order of value in the same way.

• •

118

Name _____

Exchange game

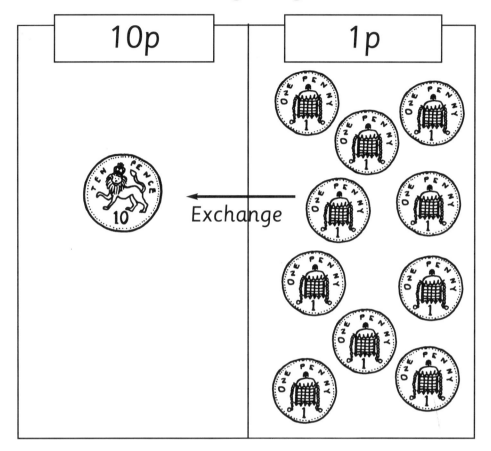

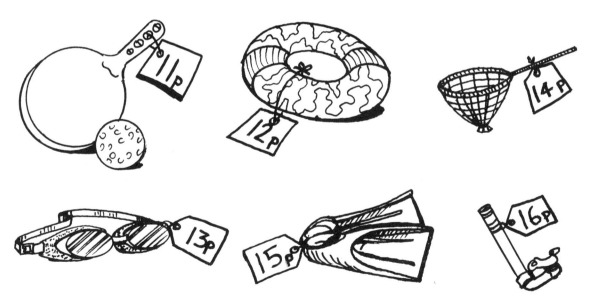

Notes for adults •

The children throw a dice and win that many pennies. When they have 10p, they exchange the pennies for a 10p. When they have over 10p, they place the coins on an item to buy it.

• •

How much money?

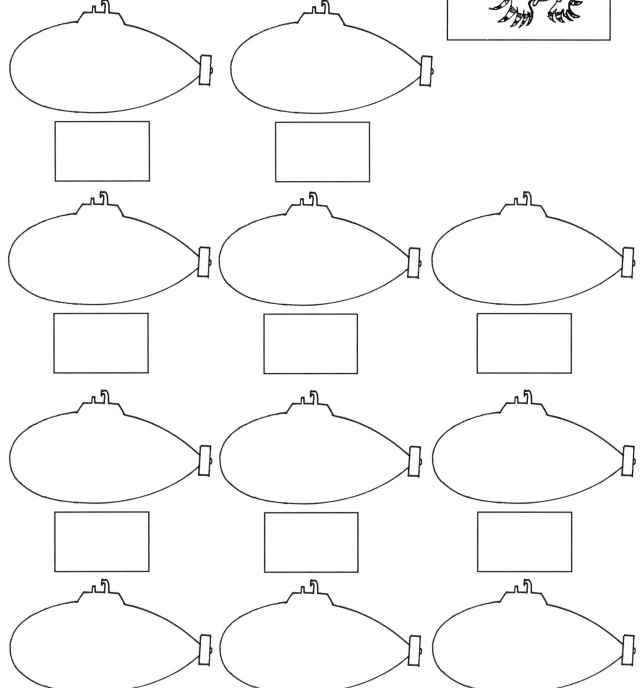

Notes for adults · Resource sheet 63

· ·

120

Pots of money

Match the money in the pots to the number lines.

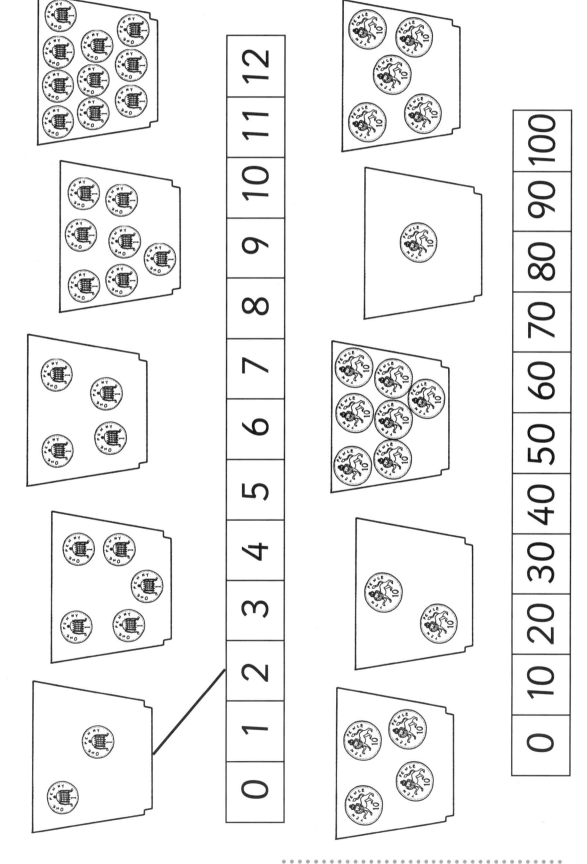

10p's and 1p's

■ How much is in each pot? Count the 10p's first.

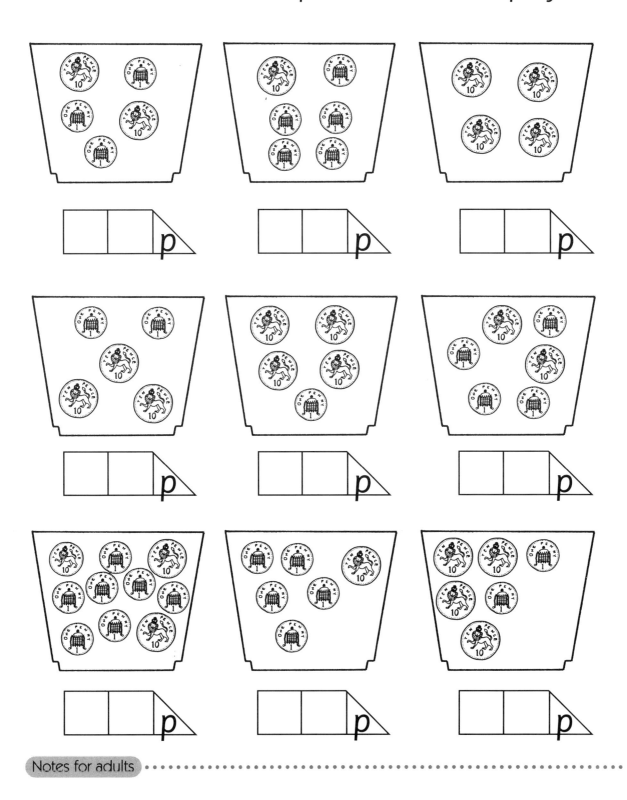

What can I buy?

I have

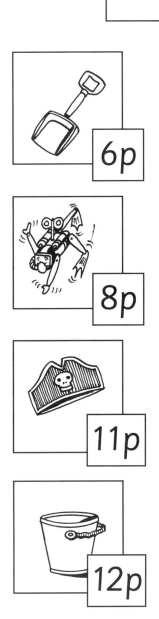

Notes for adults ●

The teacher or adult should fill in the 'I have' space with appropriate coins.
The child then draws coins next to each item they buy.

● ●

123

Counting clip art

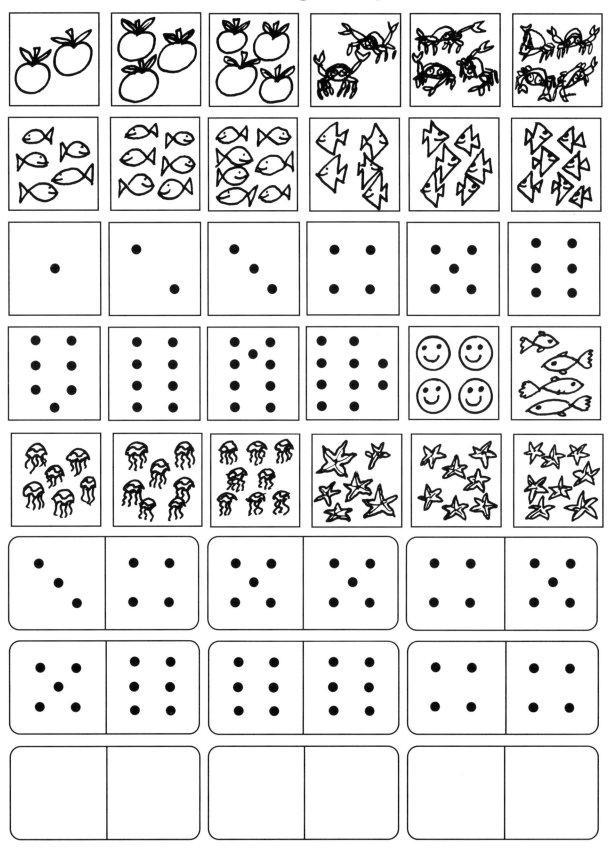

Money clip art

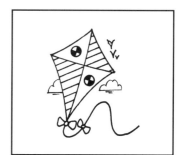

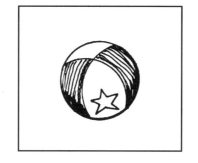

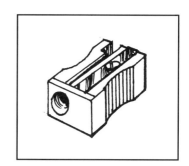

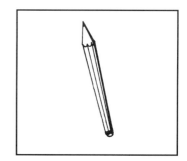

Clip art

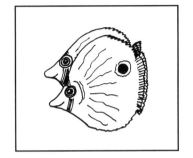

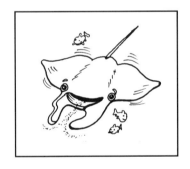

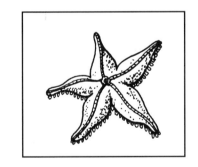

List of Assessment Focuses

Assessment focus	Chapter	Date achieved / comments
Can the child accurately count forwards/ backwards in 1's to 100 from any starting number, read the number names and reliably count objects to 10/20/100?	1	
Can the child count on 1 and count back 1 from any starting number?	1	
Can the child count in 10's to 100 and count in 10's from a number other than a multiple of 10?	1	
Can the child count back/subtract in 10's from 100 and from numbers other than multiples of 10?	1	
Can the child recognise odd and even numbers up to 100?	1	
Can the child compare numbers using greater than/ less than, fewer than/more than with numbers to 100 (and say a number that is 1 more and 10 more)?	2	
Can the child order numbers to 10/20/50/100 (and say a number that lies between)?	2	
Can the child say what each digit represents in a two-digit number and partition numbers into 10's and 1's?	2	
Does the child know the addition number facts for a given number to 10/20?	3	
Can the child add two numbers under 20 using a number line/track?	3	
Can the child understand that addition can be done in any order?	3	
Can the child add a single digit number to a multiple of 10 and see simple number patterns?	3	
Can the child add 10 and 9 using a 100 square and number line?	3	
Can the child begin to add three numbers?	3	
Can the child count back on the number line and on fingers (including crossing the 10's boundary)?	4	
Can the child understand subtraction as taking away and crossing out?	4	
Can the child recognise simple patterns in subtraction?	4	

Assessment focus	Chapter	Date achieved / comments
Can the child solve empty box problems?	5	
Can the child link counting on to addition and counting back to subtraction (and find the difference between two numbers)?	5	
Can the child halve and double numbers to 20 and use these facts for calculating?	5	
Can the child recall rapidly addition and subtraction facts?	5	
Can the child make an addition and subtraction fact from three given numbers in the 0 to 20 range?	5	
Can the child count in 2's and 10's (later 5's)?	6	
Can the child make and talk about 'lots of'?	6	
Can the child describe and make arrays and begin to see that multiplication can be done in any order?	6	
Can the child see the relationship between repeated addition and multiplication?	6	
Does the child know by heart the multiplication facts for the 2 times table?	6	
Does the child know the multiplication facts for the 10 (later 5) times table?	6	
Can the child begin to see division as repeated subtraction on the number line?	6	
Can the child recognise all coins up to £2?	7	
Can the child order coins?	7	
Can the child exchange coins?	7	
Can the child make amounts up to 10p/20/50p/£1 (and exchange coins)?	7	
Can the child solve simple shopping problems with amounts of money up to £1?	7	